HOW TO START A MEAL PREP BUSINESS

A Step-by-Step Guide to Building a Profitable Meal Prep Empire and Satisfying Hungry Customers

Mark E. Taylor

COPYRIGHT NOTICE

COPYRIGHT © 2024 Mark E. Taylor

All rights reserved. The use of any part of this book, reproduced, transmitted in any form or by any means electronic, mechanical, photocopying, recording or otherwise, or stored in a retrieval system without the prior written consent of the publisher—or in the case of photocopying or other reprographic copying, license from the Copyright Licensing agency—is an infringement of the copyright law.

TABLE OF CONTENTS

INTRODUCTION 10
    Overview of the Industry 10
    Why Start a Meal Prep Business? 12
    Understanding the Market Demand 14

CHAPTER 1 **BUSINESS PLANNING** 20
    Crafting a Business Plan 20
        Executive Summary 20
        Market Analysis 21
        Marketing Strategy 22
        Operational Plan 24
        Financial Plan 25

CHAPTER 2 **LEGAL AND REGULATORY CONSIDERATIONS** 28
    Business Structure 28
        Choosing a Legal Structure 28
        Registering Your Business 31
            Business name registration 31
            Obtaining an Employer Identification Number (EIN) ... 32
        Licenses and Permits 33
            Food handling and safety certifications 33
            Health department permits 34
            Zoning and occupancy permits 35
        Insurance 37
            General liability insurance 37
            Product liability insurance 38
            Workers' compensation 39

CHAPTER 3 **SETTING UP YOUR KITCHEN** 42
    Location and Facilities 42
        Choosing a Commercial Kitchen 42
            Renting vs. owning 42
            Shared kitchen spaces 44
        Designing Your Kitchen Layout 45
            Workflow optimization 45
            Safety and sanitation considerations 47

Equipment and Supplies 49
   Essential kitchen equipment 49
   Storage solutions 50
   Packaging materials 52

CHAPTER 4   MENU DEVELOPMENT 54
Creating a Balanced Menu 54
Nutritional Considerations 54
   Macronutrients and micronutrients 54
   Portion control 56
Dietary Preferences and Restrictions 57
   Vegan, vegetarian, gluten-free, keto, etc. 57
   Allergen management 59
Recipe Development 61
Sourcing ingredients 61
   Standardizing recipes 62
   Costing and pricing 64

CHAPTER 5   SOURCING INGREDIENTS 66
Finding Reliable Suppliers 66
Local vs. National Suppliers 66
   Pros and cons 66
Building Relationships with Suppliers 68
   Negotiating contracts 68
   Ensuring quality and consistency 69
Sustainable and Ethical Sourcing 70
   Organic and non-GMO options 70
   Fair trade and local sourcing 71

CHAPTER 6   MARKETING AND SALES 74
Building Your Brand 74
Brand Identity 74
   Logo and visual elements 74
   Brand voice and messaging 75
Online Presence 76
   Website development 76
   Social media strategy 78
Sales Channels 79
   Direct-to-consumer (DTC) 79
   Partnerships with gyms, offices, and health clubs 80
   Online marketplaces 80

CHAPTER 7   OPERATIONS AND LOGISTICS ... 82
Order Management ... 82
Order Processing Systems ... 82
- Online ordering platforms ... 82
- Subscription models ... 84

Production Scheduling ... 85
- Batch cooking ... 85
- Inventory management ... 86

Delivery and Distribution ... 87
- In-house delivery vs. third-party services ... 87
- Packaging for freshness and safety ... 89

CHAPTER 8   CUSTOMER SERVICE AND RETENTION ... 92
Building Customer Relationships ... 92
Customer Feedback ... 92
- Surveys and reviews ... 92
- Implementing feedback ... 93

Loyalty Programs ... 95
- Discounts and rewards ... 95
- Referral programs ... 96

Handling Complaints and Issues ... 97
- Effective communication ... 97
- Problem resolution strategies ... 98

CHAPTER 9   SCALING YOUR BUSINESS ... 102
Growth Strategies ... 102
Expanding Your Menu ... 102
- Seasonal offerings ... 102
- New dietary options ... 103

Geographic Expansion ... 105
- New delivery areas ... 105
- Opening additional locations ... 106

Partnerships and Collaborations ... 107
- Corporate partnerships ... 107
- Influencer collaborations ... 109

CHAPTER 10   FINANCIAL MANAGEMENT ... 112
Budgeting and Forecasting ... 112
Creating a Budget ... 112
- Fixed and variable costs ... 112
- Cash flow management ... 114

Financial Reporting. 117
Profit and loss statements 117
Balance sheets 118
Funding and Investment. 121
Bootstrapping 121
Seeking investors or loans 122

INTRODUCTION

Starting a meal prep business can be an exciting and rewarding venture. The food industry is always changing, and meal prep services have become increasingly popular in recent years. People are busier than ever, and many are looking for convenient ways to eat healthy, delicious meals without spending hours in the kitchen. This creates a great opportunity for entrepreneurs who love food and want to help others live healthier lives.

Overview of the Industry

The meal prep industry has transformed the way people approach food and nutrition. What began as a niche service has grown into a thriving sector that caters to diverse dietary needs and lifestyle preferences. To understand the current landscape, it's essential to look back at how this industry came to be.

In the past, food preparation services were primarily limited to traditional catering for events and special occasions. These businesses focused on creating large-scale meals for gatherings, rather than individual portions for daily consumption. As societal norms shifted and people's lives became busier, a gap in the market emerged for convenient, healthy meal options.

The concept of meal prep as we know it today started gaining traction in the early 2000s. This shift was driven by several factors, including increased awareness of the importance of nutrition, the rise of fitness culture, and the growing demand for time-saving solutions in daily life. Early meal prep services often catered to athletes and bodybuilders, providing carefully portioned meals with specific macronutrient ratios.

As the idea caught on, meal prep services began to expand their offerings to appeal to a broader audience. They started incorporating a wider variety of cuisines, catering to different dietary restrictions, and focusing on using high-quality, often organic ingredients. This expansion marked a significant turning point in the industry's evolution.

The advent of technology played a crucial role in the growth of meal prep businesses. Online ordering systems, mobile apps, and social media marketing allowed these companies to reach a wider customer base and streamline their operations. This technological integration made it easier for customers to customize their meals, set up recurring orders, and manage their dietary preferences with just a few clicks.

Another key milestone in the industry's development was the shift towards sustainability and eco-friendly practices. As consumers became more environmentally conscious, meal prep companies began to focus on reducing food waste, using sustainable packaging, and sourcing ingredients locally. This alignment with consumer values helped to further legitimize and grow the industry.

The COVID-19 pandemic in 2020 served as a catalyst for unprecedented growth in the meal prep sector. With restaurants closed and people spending more time at home, the demand for convenient, healthy meal options skyrocketed. Many meal prep businesses saw a surge in orders, and new companies entered the market to meet the growing demand.

The meal prep industry in 2024 is a dynamic and rapidly expanding sector. Recent market research indicates that the global meal kit delivery services market has grown significantly since 2020, with current valuations exceeding $20 billion. This remarkable growth trajectory is expected to continue, driven by factors such as increasing health consciousness, busier lifestyles, and a growing preference for home-cooked meals without the time investment of shopping and preparation.

The current market landscape is diverse, with a mix of large national brands and smaller, local operations. Some of the major players in the industry include HelloFresh, Blue Apron, and Freshly, each catering to slightly different market segments. However, there's still ample room for new entrants, particularly those focusing on niche markets or specific dietary needs.

One of the most significant trends in the current meal prep landscape is personalization. Companies are increasingly using data analytics and artificial intelligence to tailor meal recommendations based on individual preferences, dietary restrictions, and health goals. This level of customization helps to create a more engaging and satisfying experience for customers.

Another important trend is the focus on transparency and traceability in ingredient sourcing. Consumers are more interested than ever in knowing where their food comes from, and meal prep companies are responding by providing detailed information about their suppliers and production processes.

The integration of technology continues to shape the industry. Many meal prep businesses are now offering smart kitchen appliances that can be synced with their meal plans, creating a more seamless cooking experience for customers. Additionally, the use of blockchain technology for supply chain management is gaining traction, allowing for better tracking of ingredients from farm to table.

Sustainability remains a key focus, with many companies innovating in areas such as packaging materials and delivery methods to reduce their environmental impact. Some are experimenting with reusable containers, while others are optimizing delivery routes to minimize carbon emissions.

As the meal prep industry continues to evolve, it's clear that it has become an integral part of many people's lives. From its humble beginnings as a niche service for athletes to its current status as a multi-billion dollar industry, meal prep has transformed the way we think about food preparation and healthy eating.

Why Start a Meal Prep Business?

Starting a meal prep business can be an exciting and rewarding venture for aspiring entrepreneurs, especially those with a passion for food and nutrition. This section will explore the various benefits of entering this industry, as well as the personal motivations that often drive individuals to pursue this path.

One of the most attractive aspects of starting a meal prep business is the relatively low initial investment required compared to traditional food service establishments. Unlike restaurants, which often necessitate substantial upfront costs for equipment, leasing space, and hiring staff, a meal prep business can be launched with minimal overhead. Many successful meal prep entrepreneurs have started their operations from home kitchens or shared commercial spaces, allowing them to test their concept and build a customer base before committing to larger expenses.

This low barrier to entry makes the meal prep industry an accessible option for individuals who may not have the capital to open a full-scale restaurant but still want to pursue their culinary passions. It also reduces the financial risk associated with starting a new business, as the initial investment can be recouped more quickly.

Another significant advantage of a meal prep business is its inherent flexibility and scalability. Unlike traditional restaurants that are bound by their physical location and seating capacity, meal prep businesses can easily adjust their production volume to meet demand. This flexibility allows entrepreneurs to start small and gradually expand their operations as their customer base grows.

The scalability of a meal prep business also extends to its service offerings. Entrepreneurs can begin with a limited menu and expand their range of dishes over time, or they can start by catering to a specific dietary niche and later broaden their appeal to a wider audience. This adaptability enables business owners to respond quickly to market trends and customer preferences, ensuring long-term sustainability and growth.

The high demand for convenience and healthy eating options in today's fast-paced society is another compelling reason to consider starting a meal prep business. As people's lives become increasingly busy, many find it challenging to consistently prepare nutritious meals at home. This has created a significant market opportunity for businesses that can provide convenient, healthy meal solutions.

The growing awareness of the link between diet and overall health has also contributed to the demand for meal prep services. Many consumers are actively seeking ways to improve their eating habits but may lack the time or knowledge to do so effectively. A meal prep business can fill this gap by offering pre-portioned, nutritionally balanced meals that align with various dietary goals and restrictions.

Beyond these practical benefits, many individuals are drawn to the meal prep industry due to personal motivations and passions. For those with a love for cooking and nutrition, starting a meal prep business provides an opportunity to turn their hobby into a profitable venture. It allows them to express their creativity through menu development and food presentation while also sharing their culinary skills with a wider audience.

The ability to positively impact people's lives is another powerful motivator for many meal prep entrepreneurs. By providing healthy, convenient meal options, these businesses can play a role in helping individuals achieve their health and wellness goals. This sense of purpose can be incredibly fulfilling for business owners, knowing that their work is contributing to improved quality of life for their customers.

For those with a background in nutrition or dietetics, a meal prep business offers a platform to apply their expertise in a practical, impactful way. They can design menus that cater to specific health conditions or dietary requirements, providing a valuable service to individuals who may struggle to meet their nutritional needs through conventional means.

The meal prep industry also appeals to individuals with strong entrepreneurial aspirations. It offers the opportunity to build a business from the ground up, develop a unique brand, and potentially expand into multiple locations or service areas. The dynamic nature of the industry provides ample room for innovation and creativity, allowing entrepreneurs to carve out their niche in a competitive market.

Moreover, the meal prep business model lends itself well to the growing gig economy and the desire for work-life balance. Entrepreneurs can often set their own schedules, work from home (at least initially), and scale their business at a pace that suits their personal goals and lifestyle.

The potential for financial success is another motivating factor for many aspiring meal prep business owners. While profitability depends on various factors such as pricing strategy, operational efficiency, and market demand, successful meal prep businesses can generate substantial revenue. The recurring nature of meal prep services, where customers often subscribe to weekly or monthly plans, can provide a steady income stream and help with financial planning and stability.

Lastly, the meal prep industry offers opportunities for continuous learning and personal growth. Business owners must stay informed about nutrition trends, culinary techniques, food safety regulations, and business management practices. This ongoing education can be intellectually stimulating and personally rewarding for those who enjoy lifelong learning.

Understanding the Market Demand

A crucial step in starting a successful meal prep business is gaining a thorough understanding of the market demand. This involves identifying your target audience, conducting comprehensive market research, and staying attuned to consumer trends. By developing a deep understanding of these factors, you can position your business to meet the needs of your potential customers effectively.

The target audience for meal prep services is diverse and continues to expand as more people recognize the benefits of convenient, healthy meal options.

One of the primary groups that often seek out meal prep services is busy professionals. These individuals typically have demanding careers that leave little time for grocery shopping and meal preparation. They value the time-saving aspect of meal prep services, which allow them to maintain a healthy diet without sacrificing their limited free time.

For busy professionals, meal prep services offer a solution to the common dilemma of choosing between fast food and home-cooked meals. By providing nutritious, ready-to-eat options, meal prep businesses can help these individuals maintain a balanced diet even during their busiest periods. When targeting this group, it's important to emphasize the convenience factor and how your service can integrate seamlessly into their hectic lifestyles.

Another significant target audience for meal prep services is fitness enthusiasts. This group includes individuals who are actively working towards specific fitness goals, such as building muscle, losing weight, or improving athletic performance. They often have precise nutritional requirements and may struggle to consistently meet these needs through self-prepared meals.

Fitness enthusiasts appreciate meal prep services that offer customized meal plans tailored to their specific macronutrient needs. They may also be interested in services that provide detailed nutritional information for each meal, allowing them to track their intake accurately. When catering to this audience, it's beneficial to highlight how your meals can support their fitness journey and potentially offer guidance from nutrition professionals.

Families and individuals seeking convenience form another important target group for meal prep businesses. This category includes parents juggling work and childcare responsibilities, single individuals who may not enjoy cooking for one, and anyone looking to simplify their meal planning and preparation process. For these customers, meal prep services offer a way to enjoy home-style meals without the time investment of cooking from scratch every day.

When targeting families, it's important to consider offering family-sized portions or meal plans that cater to different age groups within a household. Emphasizing the variety of your menu and the ability to accommodate different taste preferences within a family can be a strong selling point.

An increasingly important segment of the meal prep market is individuals with special dietary needs. This includes people following specific diets such as vegan, vegetarian, keto, or paleo, as well as those with food allergies or intolerances. For these individuals, finding suitable meal options can be challenging and time-consuming. A meal prep service that caters to their specific dietary requirements can be invaluable.

When targeting this group, it's crucial to be transparent about ingredients and preparation methods. Offering clear labeling and the ability to easily filter meal options based on dietary restrictions can make your service particularly attractive to this audience.

To effectively serve these diverse target audiences, conducting thorough market research is essential. This process involves gathering and analyzing information about your potential customers, competitors, and the overall market landscape. By investing time and resources into market research, you can make informed decisions about your business strategy and increase your chances of success.

One effective method of market research is conducting surveys and focus groups. These tools allow you to gather direct feedback from potential customers about their preferences, pain points, and expectations regarding meal prep services. Surveys can be distributed online through social media platforms or email lists, while focus groups provide an opportunity for more in-depth discussions with a smaller group of participants.

When designing surveys or focus group questions, consider asking about factors such as preferred cuisines, dietary restrictions, ideal price points, and desired features of a meal prep service. You might also inquire about current eating habits and what would motivate them to use a meal prep service. The insights gained from these activities can guide your menu development, pricing strategy, and marketing approach.

Analyzing competitors is another crucial aspect of market research. This involves studying existing meal prep businesses in your area or target market to understand their offerings, pricing, marketing strategies, and customer base. Look at their websites, social media presence, and customer reviews to gain insights into what they're doing well and where there might be room for improvement.

Pay attention to how competitors position themselves in the market. Are they focusing on specific dietary needs, cuisines, or customer segments? This analysis can help you identify gaps in the market that your business could potentially fill.

Identifying gaps in the market is a key outcome of effective market research. These gaps represent unmet needs or underserved segments of the population that could become your niche. For example, you might discover that there's a lack of meal prep services catering to senior citizens with specific nutritional needs, or that there's demand for culturally specific cuisines that aren't currently being offered.

In addition to these targeted research methods, it's important to stay informed about broader consumer trends that could impact the meal prep industry. One significant trend is the increasing health consciousness among consumers. People are becoming more aware of the link between diet and overall health, leading to a greater demand for nutritious meal options.

This trend extends beyond just calorie counting to a more holistic view of nutrition. Consumers are interested in meals that incorporate superfoods, provide a balance of macronutrients, and support specific health goals such as boosting immunity or improving gut health. As a meal prep business owner, staying informed about nutritional science and incorporating this knowledge into your menu planning can help you appeal to health-conscious consumers.

Another important trend is the growing preference for organic and locally sourced ingredients. Consumers are increasingly concerned about the environmental impact of their food choices and the use of pesticides and artificial additives in food production. Many are willing to pay a premium for meals prepared with organic, sustainably sourced ingredients.

To capitalize on this trend, consider building relationships with local farmers and suppliers. Highlighting the use of local, organic ingredients in your marketing can be a strong selling point for environmentally conscious consumers.

The demand for customization and variety is another key trend in the meal prep industry. Consumers appreciate the ability to tailor their meal plans to their specific preferences and dietary needs. This could involve allowing customers to swap out ingredients, adjust portion sizes, or create entirely custom meal plans.

Variety is also crucial for maintaining customer interest over time. Regularly introducing new menu items, seasonal specials, or themed meal plans can help prevent menu fatigue and keep customers engaged with your service.

Lastly, it's important to note that consumer trends can vary significantly based on geographic location, demographics, and other factors. What works well in one market may not be as effective in another. This underscores the importance of conducting localized market research and staying attuned to the specific preferences and needs of your target audience.

Understanding market demand is an ongoing process. Consumer preferences and trends evolve over time, and successful meal prep businesses must be prepared to adapt accordingly. Regularly seeking feedback from your customers, staying informed about industry trends, and continuously refining your offerings based on this information can help ensure the long-term success of your meal prep business.

CHAPTER 1
BUSINESS PLANNING

Crafting a Business Plan

A well-crafted business plan serves as the foundation for your meal prep venture, guiding your decisions and helping you secure funding. Think of it as a roadmap that outlines your business's journey from concept to reality. This crucial document not only clarifies your vision but also demonstrates to potential investors or lenders that you've thoroughly considered all aspects of your business.

Executive Summary

Starting a meal prep business requires careful planning and a clear vision. The executive summary is the first and most crucial part of your business plan. It gives readers a quick overview of your entire business idea. Think of it as a short movie trailer that makes people want to see the whole film.

Your business concept is the heart of your executive summary. It explains what your meal prep business does and why it's special. For example, you might say: "Our meal prep business provides busy professionals with healthy, ready-to-eat meals delivered to their doorstep every week." This simple sentence tells people exactly what you do and who you're helping.

Next, you'll want to include your mission statement. This is a short sentence or two that explains why your business exists beyond making money. It could be something like: "We aim to make healthy eating easy and accessible for everyone, no matter how busy their lives are." Your mission statement shows that you care about more than just profits – you want to make a positive difference in people's lives.

Lastly, your executive summary should outline your vision and goals. Your vision is what you hope your business will become in the future. Maybe you want to be the leading meal prep service in your city, or perhaps you dream of expanding nationwide. Goals are more specific and measurable. For instance, you might aim to serve 1,000 customers within your first year or open a second kitchen location by year three.

Remember, the executive summary is like a first impression. It needs to be clear, exciting, and make people want to learn more about your business. Keep it short – no more than a page or two – but make sure it covers all the important points.

Market Analysis

After your executive summary, the next big part of your business plan is the market analysis. This section shows that you understand the meal prep industry and the people you want to sell to. It's like doing homework before a big test – the more you know, the better prepared you'll be.

Let's start with the industry overview. The meal prep business is part of the broader food service industry, but it's a special niche that's growing fast. In 2024, more people than ever are looking for convenient, healthy meal options. The COVID-19 pandemic changed how many people think about food, making them more interested in eating at home but not always wanting to cook from scratch.

Some interesting facts about the meal prep industry:

- It's worth billions of dollars and growing every year.
- More people are using meal prep services to save time and eat healthier.
- There's a mix of big companies and small local businesses in the industry.
- Technology is changing how meal prep businesses work, with things like app ordering and AI-powered meal planning becoming more common.

Next, you need to think about your target market and demographics. These are the specific groups of people you want to sell your meals to. For a meal prep business, your target market might include:

- Busy professionals who don't have time to cook

- People trying to lose weight or eat healthier
- Families who want convenient dinner options
- Athletes or fitness enthusiasts who need specific nutrition

For each group, think about things like:

- How old are they?
- Where do they live?
- How much money do they make?
- What are their hobbies and interests?
- What problems do they have that your meal prep service can solve?

Understanding these details helps you create meals and services that your customers will love.

The last part of your market analysis is the competitive analysis. This means looking at other meal prep businesses in your area or online. You want to know:

- Who are your main competitors?
- What do they offer?
- How much do they charge?
- What do customers like or dislike about them?
- What makes your business different or better?

You can find this information by looking at their websites, reading customer reviews, or even ordering from them to see what their service is like. This research helps you find ways to make your business stand out.

Marketing Strategy

Now that you know about your industry and customers, it's time to think about how you'll tell people about your business. This is your marketing strategy.

First, let's talk about branding and positioning. Your brand is like your business's personality. It includes things like:

- Your business name
- Your logo
- The colors and fonts you use
- The way you talk to customers

Your positioning is how you want customers to think about your business compared to others. Are you the most affordable option? The healthiest? The most convenient? For example, you might position your meal prep business as "The easiest way for busy professionals to eat healthy, home-cooked meals every day."

Next, think about your marketing channels. These are the ways you'll reach your customers. Some popular options for meal prep businesses include:

Social media: Platforms like Instagram and Facebook are great for sharing photos of your delicious meals and connecting with customers. You can post recipes, nutrition tips, and behind-the-scenes looks at your kitchen.

Search Engine Optimization (SEO): This means making your website easy to find when people search for things like "meal prep service near me" on Google. You can do this by using the right keywords on your website and creating helpful content like blog posts about healthy eating.

Partnerships: You might team up with local gyms, nutritionists, or other businesses that share your target customers. They can recommend your service to their clients, and you can offer special deals to their members.

Email marketing: Once someone tries your service, you can use email to keep in touch with them. Send them new menu items, special offers, or helpful tips about nutrition and meal planning.

Word of mouth: Happy customers telling their friends about your service can be your best marketing tool. Encourage this by offering referral bonuses or discounts for customers who bring in new business.

Your marketing strategy should also include plans for customer acquisition and retention. Acquisition means getting new customers, while retention means keeping the ones you have.

For acquisition, you might:

 - Offer a discount on the first order

 - Create a referral program where current customers get rewards for bringing in new ones

 - Run ads on social media or Google targeting your ideal customers

 For retention, consider:

 - A loyalty program that rewards repeat customers

 - Regularly asking for feedback and making improvements based on what customers say

- Offering special "members only" menu items or early access to new dishes

Remember, it often costs less to keep a current customer than to find a new one, so don't forget about retention in your marketing plans.

Operational Plan

Your operational plan explains how your meal prep business will work day-to-day. It covers all the practical details of running your business.

First, think about your location and facilities. Where will you prepare the meals? Some options include:

- Renting space in a commercial kitchen
- Converting part of your home into a certified kitchen (check local laws about this)
- Leasing a storefront with a kitchen in back

Each option has pros and cons. A commercial kitchen might be more expensive but give you more space and professional equipment. A home kitchen might be cheaper but limit how much you can produce.

You'll also need to think about storage space for ingredients and finished meals, and how you'll handle delivery or pickup.

Next, list out all the equipment and supplies you'll need. This might include:

- Commercial-grade ovens and stovetops
- Refrigerators and freezers
- Food processors and mixers
- Pots, pans, and utensils
- Storage containers for prepared meals
- Packaging materials
- Cleaning supplies

Don't forget about non-kitchen items like computers for taking orders and managing your business, or vehicles if you'll be doing deliveries.

Staffing and training is another important part of your operational plan. **Think about:**

- How many people you'll need to hire
- What roles you need to fill (chefs, prep cooks, delivery drivers, customer service)

- What skills and experience you're looking for

- How you'll train new employees

You'll want to create clear job descriptions and training manuals to make sure everyone knows what they're supposed to do. Food safety training is especially important in a meal prep business.

Your operational plan should also cover things like:

- How you'll source ingredients

- Your food preparation and packaging process

- Quality control measures

- Delivery or pickup procedures

- How you'll handle customer service and complaints

The more detailed you can be in your operational plan, the smoother your business will run once you get started.

Financial Plan

The financial plan is where you show that your meal prep business can make money. It might seem scary if you're not good with numbers, but it's really important.

Let's start with startup costs. These are all the things you need to buy or pay for before you can start selling meals. Some examples:

- Kitchen equipment

- Initial inventory of ingredients and packaging

- Rent deposit for your kitchen space

- Licenses and permits

- Insurance

- Website development

- Initial marketing costs

Make a list of everything you need and how much it will cost. This total is your startup cost.

Next, think about where this money will come from. These are your funding sources. Some options:

- Your own savings

- Loans from banks or credit unions

- Investments from friends and family
- Small business grants
- Crowdfunding campaigns

You might use a mix of these sources. Be sure to explain in your plan where you expect the money to come from.

Now for the fun part – revenue projections. This is where you estimate how much money your business will make. To do this:

1. Decide on your menu and pricing
2. Estimate how many meals you think you can sell each week
3. Multiply the number of meals by the price per meal
4. Calculate this for a month, then a year

Be realistic with your estimates. It's better to be cautious than overly optimistic.

Don't forget to factor in your costs, like ingredients, packaging, labor, and overhead expenses. Subtract these from your revenue to see your profit.

Lastly, do a break-even analysis. This shows how much you need to sell to cover all your costs. To find your break-even point:

1. Calculate your fixed costs (rent, insurance, etc.)
2. Calculate your variable costs per meal (ingredients, packaging)
3. Subtract variable costs from your meal price to get your profit per meal
4. Divide fixed costs by profit per meal

This tells you how many meals you need to sell to break even. For example, if your fixed costs are $5000 per month, and you make $5 profit per meal, you'd need to sell 1000 meals per month to break even.

Your financial plan should include projections for at least the first three years of your business. Show how you expect your revenue and profits to grow over time.

Remember, these are all estimates. Real numbers might be different, but having a solid financial plan helps you make smart decisions and shows potential investors or lenders that you've thought carefully about the money side of your business.

CHAPTER 2
LEGAL AND REGULATORY CONSIDERATIONS

Business Structure

Selecting the right business structure for your meal prep venture is a pivotal decision that will shape your company's legal and financial landscape. This choice impacts everything from your personal liability to your tax obligations, making it a critical step in establishing your business on solid ground.

Choosing a Legal Structure

When you're starting a meal prep business, one of the most important decisions you'll make is choosing the right legal structure. This choice affects how you pay taxes, your personal liability, and even how you run your business day-to-day. It's like picking the foundation for a house - you want to get it right from the start.

There are four main types of legal structures you can choose from: sole proprietorship, partnership, Limited Liability Company (LLC), and corporation. Each has its own pros and cons, and what's best for you depends on your specific situation and goals.

Let's start with the simplest option: sole proprietorship. This is when you run the business by yourself, and there's no legal separation between you and the business. It's easy to set up - in fact, if you start selling meal prep services without forming any other legal entity, you're automatically a sole proprietor.

The good things about being a sole proprietor are that it's cheap and easy to get started, and you have complete control over your business. You also get to keep all the profits. When it comes to taxes, you just report your business income on your personal tax return.

But there's a big downside: you're personally responsible for all the business debts and liabilities. If something goes wrong - like if someone gets sick from your food and sues you - they can come after your personal assets, like your house or car. That's why many food businesses choose a different structure.

Next up is partnership. This is when two or more people own and run the business together. There are two main types: general partnerships and limited partnerships. In a general partnership, all partners share in the profits, losses, and responsibilities of the business. In a limited partnership, there are both general partners (who run the business and have unlimited liability) and limited partners (who invest money but don't manage the business and have limited liability).

Partnerships can be great if you want to start a meal prep business with a friend or family member. You can combine your skills and resources. Like sole proprietorships, partnerships are relatively easy and inexpensive to form. The business doesn't pay taxes directly - instead, each partner reports their share of the business income on their personal tax return.

However, partnerships have some of the same liability issues as sole proprietorships. In a general partnership, each partner can be held personally responsible for the business debts and liabilities. Also, you have to be careful about choosing your partners, because their actions can affect you too.

Now let's talk about Limited Liability Companies, or LLCs. This is a popular choice for small businesses, including meal prep services. An LLC combines some of the best features of corporations and partnerships.

The big advantage of an LLC is right there in the name: limited liability. This means that your personal assets are protected if the business gets sued or goes into debt. You can't lose your personal savings or property because of business problems (unless you've done something illegal or irresponsible).

LLCs also offer flexibility in how they're taxed. By default, a single-member LLC is taxed like a sole proprietorship, and a multi-member LLC is taxed like a partnership. But you can choose to be taxed as a corporation if that's better for you.

Setting up an LLC is a bit more complicated and expensive than a sole proprietorship or partnership. You need to file paperwork with your state and pay filing fees. You also need to keep good records to show that your LLC is a separate entity from you personally.

Finally, we have corporations. There are two main types: C corporations and S corporations. Corporations offer the strongest protection for your personal assets, but they're also the most complex and expensive to set up and run.

In a corporation, the business is a completely separate legal entity from its owners (called shareholders). The corporation pays its own taxes, can enter into contracts, and can be sued on its own. Shareholders generally can't be held personally responsible for the corporation's debts or liabilities.

C corporations are what most people think of when they hear "corporation." They can have an unlimited number of shareholders and can offer different classes of stock. However, they face "double taxation" - the corporation pays taxes on its profits, and then shareholders pay taxes again when they receive dividends.

S corporations are a special type of corporation designed for small businesses. They avoid the double taxation issue by passing corporate income, losses, deductions, and credits through to their shareholders for federal tax purposes. However, there are limits on who can be a shareholder in an S corporation.

Corporations require more paperwork and have more rules to follow than other business structures. You need to hold regular meetings, keep detailed records, and file more complex tax returns. This can be a lot to handle for a small meal prep business just starting out.

So, which structure should you choose for your meal prep business? It depends on your specific situation. If you're just testing the waters and want to keep things simple, a sole proprietorship might be a good start. If you're working with a partner, a partnership could make sense. If you want personal asset protection without too much complexity, an LLC is often a good choice. And if you're planning a large operation with multiple investors, a corporation might be the way to go.

Remember, you can always change your business structure later if your needs change. Many successful businesses start as sole proprietorships or LLCs and then become corporations as they grow. The important thing is to think carefully about your goals, your risks, and your resources when making this decision.

It's also a good idea to talk to a lawyer or accountant before making your final choice. They can help you understand all the legal and tax implications of each business structure and choose the one that's best for your meal prep business.

Registering Your Business

Business name registration

Choosing and registering a name for your meal prep business is an exciting step. It's like giving your new venture its own identity. The name you pick will be the first thing customers see and hear about your business, so it's worth taking some time to get it right.

When you're brainstorming names, think about what makes your meal prep service special. Maybe you focus on local ingredients, or perhaps you cater to specific diets. Your name could hint at these unique features. For example, "Fresh Start Meals" might work well for a service that emphasizes healthy eating, while "Hometown Harvest Prep" could be great for a business that uses local produce.

Once you have a few ideas, it's smart to do some research. Check if anyone else is already using similar names, especially in your area or in the meal prep industry. You don't want customers getting confused between your business and someone else's.

After settling on a name, it's time to make it official. In most places, you'll need to register your business name with your state or local government. This process is often called "registering a DBA" (which stands for "Doing Business As"). Even if you're using your own name for your business, like "Jane Smith's Meal Prep," you might still need to register it.

The exact steps for registering your business name can vary depending on where you live. Usually, you'll need to fill out some forms and pay a small fee. You can often do this online through your state's Secretary of State website or your local county clerk's office.

When you register your name, you're telling the government and the public that you're the one using this name for your business. It doesn't give you exclusive rights to the name, though. For that, you'd need to look into trademarks, which is a whole different process.

Remember, if you're forming an LLC or corporation, registering your business name is often part of that process. But if you're a sole proprietor or partnership, you'll likely need to register your name separately.

Registering your business name is more than just a legal requirement. It's an important step in making your meal prep business feel real and official. It's the name you'll use on your website, your packaging, and in all your marketing.

So take your time, choose wisely, and get ready to see your business name out there in the world!

Obtaining an Employer Identification Number (EIN)

After you've chosen and registered your business name, the next important step is getting an Employer Identification Number, or EIN. Don't let the word "employer" fool you - even if you don't plan to hire any employees right away, you'll still need an EIN for your meal prep business.

Think of an EIN as a Social Security number for your business. It's a unique nine-digit number that identifies your business to the government. You'll use it for all sorts of official purposes, like filing your business taxes or opening a business bank account.

Getting an EIN is surprisingly easy and completely free. You can apply online through the Internal Revenue Service (IRS) website. The whole process usually takes just a few minutes, and you'll get your EIN right away.

To apply for an EIN, you'll need to provide some basic information about your business:

- Your business name and address
- The type of business structure you chose (like sole proprietorship, LLC, or corporation)
- The reason you're applying for an EIN (usually "Starting a new business")
- The number of employees you expect to have in the next 12 months
- The principal activity of your business (food services, in this case)

One important thing to know: the IRS prefers that you apply online, and they limit EIN applications to one per day per responsible party. So if you're starting multiple businesses, you'll need to space out your applications.

If you can't apply online for some reason, you can also apply by fax or mail using Form SS-4. But these methods take longer - several weeks for mail applications.

Now, you might be wondering why you need an EIN if you're just starting out and don't have any employees. Here are a few good reasons:

First, it helps keep your personal and business finances separate. When you use your EIN instead of your personal Social Security number for business purposes, it adds an extra layer of privacy and protection.

Second, many banks require an EIN to open a business bank account. Having a separate account for your meal prep business is crucial for keeping track of your income and expenses.

Third, if you ever decide to hire employees - even part-time helpers in the kitchen or delivery drivers - you'll need an EIN to report their wages to the IRS.

Lastly, some vendors or suppliers might ask for your EIN when you're setting up accounts with them. It's a way for them to verify that you're a legitimate business.

One more tip: once you get your EIN, keep it in a safe place. You'll be using it often throughout the life of your business. It's a good idea to store it digitally (in a secure place, of course) as well as having a physical copy.

Getting your EIN is a quick and easy step, but it's an important one in setting up your meal prep business properly. It's one of those behind-the-scenes details that helps your business run smoothly and professionally.

Licenses and Permits

Food handling and safety certifications

Starting a meal prep business means you'll be handling food that people will eat. That's a big responsibility! To make sure you're doing everything safely and correctly, you'll need to get some special certifications.

The most important one is called a Food Handler's Certificate or Food Safety Certification. It's like a driver's license, but for working with food. To get this certificate, you'll need to take a course that teaches you all about food safety. You'll learn things like:

- How to wash your hands properly (it's more than just soap and water!)
- The right temperatures for storing different types of food
- How to avoid cross-contamination (that's when bacteria from one food gets onto another)
- How to clean and sanitize your kitchen equipment

These courses usually take a few hours to complete. Some places offer them in person, but many now have online options too. At the end, you'll take a test to show you've learned the material. Don't worry - it's not too hard if you've paid attention during the course.

In most places, not only do you need this certification, but all of your employees who handle food will need it too. So if you hire kitchen staff, make sure they get certified as well.

Another certification you might need is called ServSafe. It's a bit more advanced and is often required for managers or owners of food businesses. ServSafe covers everything in the basic food handler's course, plus more about managing a safe food operation.

Getting these certifications isn't just about following the rules. It's about making sure the food you prepare is safe for your customers to eat. When you know the right way to handle food, you can feel confident that you're doing your best to keep your customers healthy.

Plus, having these certifications can make your customers feel more confident about buying from you. You can display your certifications in your kitchen or on your website to show that you take food safety seriously.

Remember, these certifications usually need to be renewed every few years. So make sure to keep track of when yours expires and get it renewed on time.

Health department permits

Now that you've got your food safety certifications, it's time to get your health department permit. This is a really important step in starting your meal prep business.

The health department is like the food safety police. They make sure that all food businesses are following the rules and keeping their kitchens clean and safe. Before you can start selling your meals, you'll need to get their approval.

To get a health department permit, you'll usually need to do a few things:

First, you'll need to fill out an application. This will ask for information about your business, like where you'll be preparing the food and what kinds of meals you'll be making.

Next, you'll probably need to submit your kitchen plans. This means drawing out where all your equipment will go, where you'll store food, where you'll wash dishes, and so on. The health department wants to make sure your kitchen is set up in a way that makes it easy to keep things clean and safe.

After that, you'll need to pay a fee. The amount can vary depending on where you live and how big your business is.

Finally, and this is the big one, you'll need to pass a health inspection. An inspector will come to your kitchen and check everything out. They'll look at things like:

- How do you store your food (Is it at the right temperature? Is it protected from contamination?)
- How you clean your equipment and utensils
- If you have proper handwashing stations
- How you handle raw ingredients to avoid spreading bacteria

The inspector might also ask you questions about your food safety practices. This is where all that knowledge from your food safety certification comes in handy!

If you pass the inspection, great! You'll get your permit and can start cooking. If not, don't worry too much. The inspector will tell you what needs to be fixed, and you can make those changes and have them come back for another look.

One important thing to know: health inspections don't stop after you get your initial permit. The health department will continue to inspect your kitchen regularly to make sure you're keeping up with food safety standards. So always be prepared for a surprise visit!

Getting your health department permit might seem like a lot of work, but it's really important. It helps ensure that you're running a safe operation, which protects both your customers and your business.

Zoning and occupancy permits

The last set of permits you'll need to think about are zoning and occupancy permits. These might sound a bit boring, but they're super important for making sure your meal prep business is operating legally in the right place.

Let's start with zoning permits. Zoning is all about what kinds of businesses can operate in different areas of a city or town. It's like having different neighborhoods for different types of buildings and businesses.

Before you set up your meal prep kitchen, you need to make sure that the area you want to use is zoned for food businesses. Some areas are only for homes, some are for shops, and some are for factories. You need to be in an area that allows food preparation businesses.

To get a zoning permit, you'll need to go to your local city or county planning office. Tell them about your meal prep business and where you want to set it up. They'll check if it's allowed in that area. If it is, great! If not, you might need to look for a different location.

Sometimes, you might be able to get a special exception or variance if your business doesn't quite fit the usual zoning rules. But this can be a long process and isn't guaranteed to work.

Now, let's talk about occupancy permits. An occupancy permit (sometimes called a certificate of occupancy) says that a building is safe for people to use for business.

To get an occupancy permit, your building will need to pass inspections to make sure it meets safety codes. This includes things like:

- Having proper fire exits
- Making sure the electrical system is safe
- Having enough bathrooms for the number of people who will be working there
- Making sure the building is structurally sound

If you're renting a space for your meal prep business, the building might already have an occupancy permit. But you'll still need to make sure it's valid for the type of business you're running. A permit for an office might not cover a commercial kitchen, for example.

If you're setting up your kitchen in a new building or making major changes to an existing one, you'll definitely need to get a new occupancy permit.

Getting these permits might seem like a hassle, but they're really important. They help make sure your business is safe for you, your employees, and your customers. They also protect you legally. If you're operating without the right permits and something goes wrong, you could get in big trouble.

One last tip: start the process of getting these permits early. It can sometimes take a while, especially if you need to make changes to your plans or your building. You don't want to be ready to start your business but have to wait because you're still working on permits!

Remember, the exact rules for these permits can vary depending on where you live. So it's always a good idea to check with your local government offices to find out exactly what you need for your meal prep business. They can guide you through the process and make sure you don't miss anything important.

Insurance

General liability insurance

When you're starting a meal prep business, getting the right insurance is super important. It's like having a safety net that catches you if something goes wrong. One of the most important types of insurance you'll need is called general liability insurance.

General liability insurance protects your business if someone gets hurt because of your business activities or if you accidentally damage someone else's property. It's like a shield that helps protect you from having to pay a lot of money if something bad happens.

Here are some examples of what general liability insurance might cover:

Imagine a delivery driver slips and falls while dropping off meals at a customer's house. If the driver gets hurt, your general liability insurance could help pay for their medical bills.

Or maybe you're cooking in a rented kitchen and accidentally start a small fire that damages some equipment. Your general liability insurance could help pay to fix or replace the damaged items.

Another situation could be if a customer claims they got food poisoning from one of your meals. Even if it wasn't your fault, they might try to sue you. General liability insurance could help pay for a lawyer to defend you and cover any money you might have to pay the customer.

When you're shopping for general liability insurance, you'll need to decide how much coverage you want. This is called the policy limit. It's the maximum amount the insurance company will pay if something happens. A common limit for small businesses is $1 million, but you might need more or less depending on your specific business.

The cost of general liability insurance can vary a lot. It depends on things like:

- How big your business is
- What kind of food you're preparing
- Where your business is located
- How much coverage you want

You might pay anywhere from a few hundred to a few thousand dollars a year for this insurance. It might seem like a lot of money, but it's way less than what you might have to pay if something goes wrong and you don't have insurance.

When you're getting quotes for general liability insurance, make sure to shop around. Different insurance companies might offer different prices for the same coverage. It's also a good idea to talk to an insurance agent who knows about food businesses. They can help you figure out exactly what kind of coverage you need.

Remember, having general liability insurance isn't just about protecting your business financially. It also shows your customers that you're responsible and prepared. Some clients, especially if you're catering to businesses or events, might even require you to have this insurance before they'll work with you.

In the world of meal prep businesses, where you're handling food that people will eat, having good insurance is super important. General liability insurance is a key part of keeping your business safe and successful.

Product liability insurance

Now let's talk about another really important type of insurance for your meal prep business: product liability insurance. This is a special kind of insurance that protects you if the food you make causes problems for your customers.

Think about it: you're making food that people are going to eat. Even if you're super careful and follow all the safety rules, there's always a tiny chance that something could go wrong. That's where product liability insurance comes in.

Here's an example of how it works: Let's say someone eats one of your meals and gets really sick. They might have to go to the hospital and miss work. If they think it was because of your food, they might try to sue your business to get money for their medical bills and lost wages. Product liability insurance could help pay for your legal defense and any money you might have to pay to the customer.

Product liability insurance doesn't just cover cases of food poisoning. It can also help if someone has an allergic reaction to your food, or if they're hurt by something in the food (like if a piece of plastic accidentally got into a meal during packaging).

One thing that makes product liability insurance extra important for meal prep businesses is that your food might be eaten days after you prepare it. If something goes wrong with the food during that time, you could still be held responsible.

When you're looking at product liability insurance, you'll need to decide on a coverage limit, just like with general liability insurance. The amount you need can depend on things like:

- How many meals you're making each week

- What kinds of ingredients you're using (some foods are riskier than others)

- Who your customers are (if you're selling to businesses or institutions, you might need more coverage)

The cost of product liability insurance can vary a lot. It might be included in a package with your general liability insurance, or you might need to buy it separately. Either way, it's a good idea to talk to an insurance agent who knows about food businesses to make sure you're getting the right coverage.

One way to possibly lower your insurance costs is to have really good safety and quality control procedures in your kitchen. If you can show the insurance company that you're doing everything possible to prevent problems, they might offer you a better rate.

Some meal prep business owners wonder if they really need product liability insurance if they already have general liability insurance. The answer is usually yes. While general liability insurance covers a lot of things, product liability insurance is specifically designed to protect you from problems with the food you make. It's an extra layer of protection that's really important in the food business.

Having product liability insurance isn't just about protecting your business financially. It also shows your customers that you take food safety seriously and that you're prepared to take responsibility if something goes wrong. This can help build trust with your customers, which is super important for any food business.

Remember, the goal is never to have to use your insurance. But having good product liability coverage gives you peace of mind. You can focus on making great meals for your customers, knowing that you're protected if something unexpected happens.

Workers' compensation

The last type of insurance we need to talk about is workers' compensation. This is a special kind of insurance that helps protect your employees if they get hurt or sick because of their job.

Now, you might be thinking, "But I don't have any employees yet!" That's okay. It's still good to know about workers' compensation because you'll probably need it as your meal prep business grows.

Here's how workers' compensation works: If one of your employees gets hurt while working for you, this insurance helps pay for their medical bills and some of their lost wages while they can't work. It's like a safety net for your workers.

Let's say you hire someone to help in the kitchen. One day, they slip on a wet floor and hurt their back. Workers' compensation would help pay for their doctor visits, any medicine they need, and some of their salary while they're recovering and can't work.

Workers' compensation doesn't just cover accidents. It can also help if someone gets sick because of their job. For example, if someone develops carpal tunnel syndrome from chopping vegetables all day, workers' compensation might cover their treatment.

In most states, if you have employees, you're required by law to have workers' compensation insurance. The exact rules can be different depending on where you live. Some states require it as soon as you hire your first employee, while others might not require it until you have a certain number of employees.

The cost of workers' compensation insurance depends on a few things:

  - How many employees you have

  - What kind of work they do (kitchen work is usually considered more risky than office work)

  - Your history of workplace accidents (if you're just starting out, you won't have a history yet)

You might pay anywhere from a few hundred to a few thousand dollars a year for workers' compensation, depending on these factors.

One important thing to know: in most cases, workers' compensation covers your employees even if an accident was their fault. For example, if someone cuts themselves because they weren't being careful with a knife, workers' compensation would still help them. This protects both you and your employees from the costs of workplace accidents.

Having workers' compensation insurance is good for your business in a few ways:

  - It helps you follow the law, which is always important.

  - It shows your employees that you care about their safety and well-being.

  - It protects your business from lawsuits. In most cases, if an employee accepts workers' compensation benefits, they can't sue your business for the same injury.

When you're ready to get workers' compensation insurance, you have a few options. In some states, you have to buy it from a state-run program. In others, you can buy it from private insurance companies. Some small business insurance packages include workers' compensation along with other types of insurance.

As your meal prep business grows and you start hiring people, make sure to add workers' compensation to your insurance plan. It's an important part of being a responsible business owner and taking care of the people who help make your business successful.

Remember, creating a safe work environment is the best way to avoid needing to use your workers' compensation insurance. Make sure to train your employees well, keep your kitchen clean and organized, and always put safety first. That way, everyone stays healthy and happy, and your meal prep business can keep growing and thriving.

CHAPTER 3
SETTING UP YOUR KITCHEN

Location and Facilities

The heart of your meal prep business beats in your kitchen. Choosing the right location and setting up an efficient, compliant facility is crucial to your operation's success.

Choosing a Commercial Kitchen

Renting vs. owning

When you're starting a meal prep business, one of the biggest decisions you'll face is where to set up your kitchen. You have two main options: renting a kitchen space or buying your own. Both choices have their good points and challenges, so let's break them down.

Renting a kitchen space is often the go-to choice for new meal prep businesses. It's like renting an apartment instead of buying a house. When you rent, you don't need as much money to get started. You pay a monthly fee to use the kitchen, which is usually much less than what you'd spend to buy and set up your own kitchen.

Renting also gives you more flexibility. If your business grows quickly, you can often move to a bigger space without too much trouble. Or if things don't work out as planned, you're not stuck with a kitchen you own but can't use.

Another good thing about renting is that the landlord usually takes care of maintenance and repairs. If an oven breaks down or the plumbing gets clogged, it's typically not your problem to fix. This can save you a lot of headaches and unexpected costs.

However, renting has some downsides too. You might have to share the kitchen with other businesses, which means you can't always use it when you want. You also can't make big changes to the kitchen setup without the landlord's permission. And over time, the cost of rent can add up to more than what you might have spent to buy a kitchen.

Now, let's talk about owning your kitchen. Buying a kitchen space is a big investment, but it can pay off in the long run. When you own your kitchen, you have complete control over the space. You can set it up exactly how you want, use it whenever you need to, and make changes as your business grows.

Owning also means you're building equity. Every payment you make is an investment in your business, not just money going to a landlord. And if you decide to sell your business someday, owning the kitchen can make it more valuable.

But owning comes with responsibilities too. You'll need to handle all the maintenance and repairs yourself. If something breaks, you're the one who has to fix it or pay to have it fixed. You'll also need to pay property taxes and insurance, which can be expensive.

The biggest challenge with owning is the upfront cost. Buying a commercial kitchen requires a lot of money. You might need to take out a big loan, which can be scary when you're just starting out.

So, how do you decide between renting and owning? Here are some questions to ask yourself:

- How much money do you have to start your business?

- How sure are you about the size of kitchen you'll need in the long term?

- Are you ready for the responsibilities of owning property?

- How important is it to you to have complete control over your kitchen space?

If you're just starting out and aren't sure how big your business will get, renting might be the safer choice. You can always switch to owning later when you have a better idea of what you need.

On the other hand, if you have the money available and you're confident about your long-term plans, owning could be a smart investment.

Remember, there's no one-size-fits-all answer. The right choice depends on your specific situation, your goals, and how comfortable you are with risk.

Take your time to think it through and maybe talk to other meal prep business owners about what worked for them.

Shared kitchen spaces

Now, let's talk about a special type of renting option that's becoming more and more popular for meal prep businesses: shared kitchen spaces. These are also sometimes called commercial kitchens or commissary kitchens.

A shared kitchen space is like a big kitchen that many different food businesses can use. Think of it as a gym, but for cooking instead of exercising. Just like how a gym has different equipment that members can use, a shared kitchen has all the cooking equipment and storage space that food businesses need.

Here's how it usually works: You pay a fee to become a member of the shared kitchen. This fee might be monthly, or you might pay by the hour for the time you use. Then, you get to use the kitchen facilities during your scheduled times.

These shared kitchens come with a lot of benefits, especially for new meal prep businesses. First, they're usually much cheaper than renting your own kitchen. All the expensive equipment like big ovens, mixers, and refrigerators are already there for you to use. You don't have to buy them yourself, which saves you a ton of money when you're just starting out.

Shared kitchens also often come with other helpful features. Many have storage spaces where you can keep your ingredients and supplies. Some even offer office spaces or meeting rooms where you can do the business side of your work.

Another big plus of shared kitchens is the community. You're working alongside other food entrepreneurs. This can be great for networking, sharing tips, and maybe even collaborating on projects. It's like having a bunch of coworkers, even though you're running your own business.

Shared kitchens are also usually fully licensed and inspected. This means you don't have to worry about meeting all the health department requirements on your own. The kitchen takes care of a lot of that for you.

But, like anything, shared kitchens have some downsides too. The biggest one is that you have to work around other people's schedules. You might not always get the exact times you want to use the kitchen. This can be tricky if you have big orders or if you prefer to work at specific times.

Also, while shared kitchens provide the big equipment, you usually need to bring your own smaller tools and supplies. And you always need to clean up thoroughly after yourself, to keep the space nice for the next user.

Another thing to think about is that in a shared kitchen, you don't have as much control over the space as you would in your own kitchen. You can't rearrange things or make big changes to suit your specific needs.

So, how do you decide if a shared kitchen is right for your meal prep business? Here are some things to consider:

- How much kitchen time do you need each week?
- What times of day do you prefer to work?
- How important is it to you to have your own permanent space?
- Do you like the idea of working around other food businesses?
- How much money can you afford to spend on kitchen space?

If you're just starting out, a shared kitchen can be a great way to get your business off the ground without spending too much money. It gives you a professional space to work in and lets you focus on perfecting your meals and building your customer base.

As your business grows, you might find that you outgrow the shared kitchen. That's okay! Many successful food businesses start in shared kitchens and then move to their own spaces when they're ready.

To find shared kitchens in your area, try searching online for "commercial kitchens" or "commissary kitchens" plus your city name. You can also ask other local food business owners if they know of any good options.

When you're checking out shared kitchens, make sure to visit in person if you can. Look at the equipment they have, ask about their scheduling system, and try to get a feel for the community of businesses using the space.

Designing Your Kitchen Layout

The heart of any meal prep business beats in its kitchen. A well-designed kitchen layout is crucial for smooth operations, efficiency, and food safety. Let's look at two key aspects of kitchen design: workflow optimization and safety and sanitation considerations.

Workflow optimization

When you're setting up your meal prep kitchen, thinking about workflow is super important. Workflow is all about how you and your team move around the kitchen while you're working. A good workflow makes your job easier and faster, while a bad one can slow you down and make things frustrating.

Think of your kitchen like a race track. You want to be able to zoom around smoothly, not keep stopping and starting or bumping into things. In kitchen terms, this means setting things up so you can move from one task to the next without wasting time or energy.

Let's break down the main areas you'll have in your meal prep kitchen:

Storage area: This is where you keep your ingredients and supplies.

Prep area: Here's where you wash, chop, and get ingredients ready.

Cooking area: This is where your stoves and ovens are.

Packaging area: This is where you put the finished meals into containers.

Cleaning area: Your sinks and dishwashing station go here.

The trick is to arrange these areas in a way that makes sense for how you'll use them. You want to create a smooth path from start to finish.

A common setup is to have your workflow move in a circle. You might start at the storage area to get your ingredients, then move to the prep area to get everything ready. From there, you go to the cooking area to make the meals. Once they're cooked, you move to the packaging area to put them in containers. Finally, you end up at the cleaning area to wash up.

This circular flow helps you avoid crossing paths or having to backtrack, which can slow you down and increase the chance of accidents.

Here are some tips for good workflow:

Put your prep area close to your storage area. This way, you don't have to walk far with heavy ingredients.

Keep your cooking area near your prep area. You don't want to be running across the kitchen with chopped vegetables or raw meat.

Have your packaging area close to where the finished food comes out. If you're packaging hot meals, you want them to stay hot.

Make sure there's enough space between different stations. You don't want people bumping into each other while they work.

Think about where you'll put trash cans and recycling bins. You want them to be easy to reach but not in the way.

Consider having a separate area for dry storage (like spices and canned goods) and cold storage (your refrigerators and freezers).

Remember, the perfect layout depends on what kind of meals you're making and how many people will be working in the kitchen. If you're just starting out, you might not need a huge space with separate areas for everything. But thinking about workflow from the beginning can help you set up a kitchen that grows with your business.

It's a good idea to draw out your kitchen layout on paper before you start moving things around. You can use simple shapes to represent different pieces of equipment and try different arrangements. Some people even cut out paper shapes and move them around on a bigger sheet to see what works best.

Don't be afraid to make changes if something isn't working. Your kitchen layout isn't set in stone. As you start working, you might notice ways to improve the flow. Maybe you find yourself always running to the other side of the kitchen for a certain tool, or you realize two people are always bumping into each other in one spot. Pay attention to these things and be ready to adjust your layout.

A well-designed kitchen with good workflow will help you work faster, make fewer mistakes, and keep your team happy. It might take some time to get it just right, but it's worth the effort. A smooth-running kitchen is key to a successful meal prep business!

Safety and sanitation considerations

When you're designing your meal prep kitchen, safety and sanitation are super important. They're not just about following rules – they're about keeping your customers healthy and your business running smoothly.

Let's start with safety. A safe kitchen is one where people don't get hurt. Here are some key things to think about:

Floors: Your kitchen floor should be non-slip, even when it's wet. This helps prevent falls, which are a common accident in kitchens. Make sure there are no uneven spots or loose tiles that people could trip on.

Lighting: Good lighting is crucial for safety. You need to be able to see clearly to avoid accidents and to make sure food is cooked properly. Make sure all areas of your kitchen are well-lit, especially prep areas and around equipment.

Fire safety: Keep fire extinguishers in easy-to-reach spots and make sure everyone knows how to use them. Don't put anything flammable near your stoves or ovens.

Equipment placement: Leave enough space around equipment so people can move safely. Don't put hot appliances like ovens right next to cold ones like refrigerators – this can make both work harder and increase the risk of breakdowns.

Electrical safety: Make sure you have enough outlets so you're not overloading any one circuit. Keep electrical equipment away from water sources.

Now let's talk about sanitation. In a meal prep kitchen, keeping things clean is crucial. Here's what to consider:

Handwashing stations: You need plenty of sinks for handwashing. Put them in convenient spots so it's easy for everyone to wash their hands often.

Surface materials: Choose materials for your countertops and work surfaces that are easy to clean and sanitize. Stainless steel is popular in commercial kitchens because it's durable and easy to keep clean.

Storage: Store food and equipment off the ground. This makes it easier to clean underneath and helps prevent pest problems.

Waste management: Have separate bins for trash, recycling, and compost. Keep them away from food prep areas to avoid contamination.

Cleaning equipment storage: Have a designated spot to store cleaning supplies. Keep them separate from food and food prep equipment.

Ventilation: Good airflow helps control temperature and humidity, which can affect food safety. It also helps remove cooking odors and smoke.

Here are some general tips that cover both safety and sanitation:

Create separate zones for different tasks. This helps prevent cross-contamination. For example, keep raw meat prep separate from areas where you handle cooked food or fresh produce.

Use color-coding. Many kitchens use different colored cutting boards or utensils for different types of food. For example, red for raw meat, green for vegetables, and white for dairy.

Install a good ventilation system. This helps control temperature and humidity, removes cooking odors, and keeps the air clean.

Plan for easy cleaning. Avoid creating hard-to-reach spots where dirt and grime can build up. Make sure you can move equipment for thorough cleaning.

Consider flow when placing sinks and sanitizing stations. You want to encourage good habits by making it convenient for staff to wash hands and clean equipment.

Leave space for a first aid kit and emergency procedures poster. Everyone should know where these are and how to use them.

Remember, your local health department will have specific rules about kitchen safety and sanitation. Make sure you know these rules and follow them when designing your kitchen. They might have requirements about things like the number of sinks you need or the type of materials you can use for different surfaces.

It's a good idea to have a professional kitchen designer or a health inspector look at your plans before you start building or renovating. They can spot potential problems and suggest improvements.

Creating a safe and sanitary kitchen might seem like a lot of work, but it's one of the most important things you can do for your meal prep business. It protects your customers, your employees, and your business reputation. Plus, a well-designed kitchen that prioritizes safety and sanitation is often more efficient and pleasant to work in. It's an investment that pays off in many ways!

Equipment and Supplies

Essential kitchen equipment

Setting up your meal prep kitchen with the right equipment is like giving a superhero their superpowers. The right tools can make your job easier, faster, and help you create amazing meals for your customers. Let's talk about the must-have equipment for your meal prep business.

First up, you'll need a good range or cooktop. This is where the magic happens! For a meal prep business, you'll want a commercial-grade stove with multiple burners. Gas stoves are popular in professional kitchens because they give you quick, precise control over heat. But if gas isn't an option, electric stoves can work well too.

Next to your stove, you'll want at least one oven, maybe more depending on how many meals you're making. Convection ovens are great for meal prep because they cook food evenly and often faster than regular ovens. Some meal prep kitchens also use combi ovens, which can steam and roast food.

For quick cooking and reheating, a microwave or two can be really handy. Look for commercial-grade microwaves that can handle heavy use.

Now, let's talk about cold storage. You'll need refrigerators to keep ingredients fresh and store prepared meals. Commercial refrigerators come in different sizes, from small under-counter models to walk-in coolers. Choose based on how much food you'll be storing. Don't forget about freezers too, especially if you'll be offering frozen meals or storing ingredients long-term.

For food prep, a good set of knives is essential. You'll want chef's knives, paring knives, and maybe a few specialty knives depending on what you cook.

Remember, sharp knives are safer than dull ones, so invest in a good knife sharpener too.

Cutting boards are the partners to your knives. Have several in different sizes, and consider color-coding them to prevent cross-contamination (like using red boards for raw meat and green for vegetables).

You'll need lots of pots and pans. Stock pots for soups and sauces, sauté pans for quick cooking, and baking sheets for roasting vegetables or baking. Non-stick pans can be helpful for some dishes, but stainless steel is great for most cooking tasks.

A food processor is a real time-saver for chopping, slicing, and pureeing. If you'll be making a lot of smoothies or sauces, a high-powered blender is worth the investment.

For measuring ingredients accurately, you'll need measuring cups and spoons, as well as a good kitchen scale. Precise measurements are key to consistent meals.

Don't forget about smaller tools like vegetable peelers, can openers, thermometers, and tongs. These might seem minor, but you'll use them all the time.

If you're going to be cooking a lot of rice or grains, a rice cooker can be a big help. They're not just for rice – you can use them for quinoa, barley, and other grains too.

For mixing batters or doughs, a stand mixer is really useful. You can also get attachments for stand mixers that do all sorts of tasks, like grinding meat or making pasta.

Lastly, think about cleaning equipment. You'll need a good dishwasher (or several) to keep up with all the dishes. A three-compartment sink is standard in commercial kitchens for washing, rinsing, and sanitizing.

Remember, you don't have to buy everything at once. Start with the essentials and add more as your business grows. And don't forget to maintain your equipment properly. Regular cleaning and maintenance will keep your kitchen running smoothly and help your equipment last longer.

Storage solutions

Good storage is like having a well-organized closet – it makes your life so much easier! In a meal prep kitchen, smart storage solutions help you keep ingredients fresh, work efficiently, and stay organized. Let's look at some great storage ideas for your business.

First, let's talk about dry storage. This is where you'll keep things like spices, grains, and canned goods. Shelving units are your best friend here. Look for sturdy, adjustable shelves that you can customize to fit different sized items. Metal shelving is popular in commercial kitchens because it's strong and easy to clean.

For your dry goods, clear, airtight containers are fantastic. They keep ingredients fresh and let you see at a glance what you have and how much is left. Label everything clearly with the name of the item and the date you opened it.

Now, onto cold storage. Your refrigerators and freezers are crucial for keeping perishable ingredients fresh. Inside these, use clear plastic bins to keep similar items together. For example, you might have a bin for dairy products, another for prepped vegetables, and so on.

In your freezer, consider using a labeling system with different colored labels for different types of food. This can help you quickly find what you need, even when things are frosty.

For your prepped ingredients, invest in a good set of food storage containers. Look for ones that are sturdy, stackable, and come in various sizes. Many professional kitchens use clear polycarbonate containers because they're durable and let you see what's inside.

Don't forget about vertical space! Wall-mounted racks or pegboards can be great for storing pots, pans, and utensils. This keeps them easy to reach and frees up valuable counter and cabinet space.

For your spices and herbs, a spice rack or drawer insert can keep these small items organized and easy to find. Some kitchens use magnetic strips on the wall to hold small metal spice containers.

If you have the space, a walk-in cooler or freezer can be a game-changer for a meal prep business. These give you lots of storage space and make it easy to organize large quantities of ingredients or prepared meals.

For items you use all the time, like cooking oils or frequently used spices, consider setting up a small shelf or cart near your cooking area. This puts these items within easy reach while you're working.

Remember to think about food safety when planning your storage. Raw ingredients should always be stored below cooked or ready-to-eat foods to prevent cross-contamination. And make sure you have a system for rotating stock so that older ingredients get used first.

Lastly, don't forget about storage for non-food items. You'll need a place to keep cleaning supplies (separate from food storage areas), a spot for extra packaging materials, and maybe even some office storage for paperwork and records.

Good storage solutions might not seem as exciting as fancy cooking equipment, but they're just as important for running a smooth, efficient meal prep kitchen. With the right storage setup, you'll save time, reduce waste, and keep your kitchen organized and clean.

Packaging materials

Packaging might not be the first thing you think about when starting a meal prep business, but it's super important! Good packaging keeps your food fresh, makes it look appealing, and helps your customers enjoy their meals. Let's talk about the different packaging materials you might need.

First up, let's consider containers for individual meals. These come in all shapes and sizes, but for meal prep, rectangular containers with compartments are popular. They let you separate different parts of the meal and make portion control easy. Look for containers that are microwave-safe and dishwasher-safe, so your customers can easily reheat and clean them.

You have a few material options for these containers. Plastic is lightweight and inexpensive, but make sure you choose BPA-free plastic that can handle being heated. Glass containers are another option. They're more expensive, but they're very durable and some customers prefer them because they can be heated in the oven as well as the microwave.

For customers who want to transfer their meals to their own plates, you might consider disposable containers. If you go this route, look into eco-friendly options like containers made from recycled materials or biodegradable plastics.

Don't forget about lids! You want lids that seal tightly to keep food fresh and prevent spills. Some containers come with snap-on lids, while others have lids that can be heat-sealed for extra security.

If you're offering soups or sauces, you'll need containers that are leak-proof. Look for containers with screw-on lids or strong seals.

For salads or meals where you want to keep some ingredients separate until eating time, consider containers with removable inserts or small separate containers for dressings or toppings.

Now, let's talk about bags. If you're delivering meals or if customers are picking them up to take home, you'll need sturdy bags to put the containers in. Paper bags can work, but for hot meals, insulated bags are better at keeping food at the right temperature. Some meal prep businesses use reusable insulated bags that customers return each week.

Labels are another important part of packaging. You'll need labels to show what each meal is, when it was prepared, and any heating instructions. If you're including nutritional information, that goes on the label too. Look for labels that stick well to your containers and can handle being in the refrigerator or freezer.

If you're packaging hot meals, you might want to use heat-seal film over your containers before putting the lids on. This helps keep the food hot and fresh.

For businesses offering weekly meal plans, some use large, reusable cooler bags to deliver all of a customer's meals at once. These can be a bit pricey upfront, but they're great for keeping food cold during delivery and customers often appreciate the eco-friendly approach.

Don't forget about smaller packaging items like sauce cups for dressings or dips, and cutlery if you're offering that as part of your service.

Lastly, think about branding. Your packaging is a great place to showcase your logo and brand colors. This helps make your meals recognizable and can be a form of marketing when customers take their meals to work or school.

When choosing your packaging, consider your budget, your brand image, and what's most practical for your meals and your customers. It's okay to start simple and upgrade your packaging as your business grows.

Remember, packaging isn't just about looks – it's about functionality too. The right packaging keeps your food safe and fresh, makes it easy for customers to enjoy their meals, and can even help reduce food waste. Take some time to find the packaging that works best for your unique meal prep business.

CHAPTER 4
MENU DEVELOPMENT

Creating a Balanced Menu
Nutritional Considerations

The menu is the heart and soul of your meal prep business. It's not just about creating delicious dishes; it's about crafting a well-rounded, nutritious, and appealing selection that caters to a diverse range of tastes and dietary needs.

Macronutrients and micronutrients

When you're running a meal prep business, understanding nutrition is like having a secret superpower. It helps you create meals that not only taste good but also make your customers feel great. Let's break down the basics of macronutrients and micronutrients in a way that's easy to understand and apply to your meal planning.

First, let's talk about macronutrients. These are the big three nutrients that our bodies need in large amounts: proteins, carbohydrates, and fats. Think of them as the main ingredients in the recipe of good health.

Proteins are like the building blocks of our body. They help repair tissues, make enzymes and hormones, and keep our immune system strong. Good sources of protein include meat, fish, eggs, dairy, beans, and tofu. When you're planning meals, try to include a good protein source in each one. For example, you might add grilled chicken to a salad or use lentils in a vegetarian curry.

Carbohydrates are our body's main source of energy. They're like the fuel that keeps our engine running. There are two main types of carbs: simple and complex. Simple carbs are found in things like fruits and sugar. They give quick energy but don't last long. Complex carbs, found in whole grains, vegetables, and legumes, provide longer-lasting energy. In your meal prep, focus on including more complex carbs. For instance, you could use brown rice instead of white rice, or add sweet potatoes to a dish.

Fats often get a bad rap, but they're actually really important for our health. They help our body absorb certain vitamins, keep our skin healthy, and make us feel full. The key is to focus on healthy fats, like those found in avocados, nuts, seeds, and olive oil. When you're cooking, try using olive oil instead of butter, or add some sliced avocado to a sandwich.

Now, let's move on to micronutrients. These are nutrients that our body needs in smaller amounts, but they're just as important. Vitamins and minerals fall into this category. Think of micronutrients as the special ingredients that make a recipe pop.

Vitamins help our body in all sorts of ways. For example, Vitamin C helps our immune system, while Vitamin D is important for strong bones. You can get vitamins from a wide range of foods. Fruits and vegetables are especially good sources. When you're planning meals, try to include a variety of colorful fruits and veggies. The more colors on the plate, the more different vitamins your customers are likely to get.

Minerals are another type of micronutrient. They do things like help build strong bones (calcium), carry oxygen in our blood (iron), and regulate our heartbeat (potassium). Different foods are rich in different minerals. For instance, leafy greens are great for iron, dairy products provide calcium, and bananas are high in potassium.

When you're planning meals for your prep business, try to create a balance of all these nutrients. A good rule of thumb is to fill half the plate with fruits and vegetables, a quarter with lean protein, and a quarter with complex carbohydrates. Then, add some healthy fats in the cooking process or as a topping.

Remember, everyone's nutritional needs are a bit different. Some of your customers might be athletes who need more protein, while others might be trying to lose weight and want meals lower in calories. It's a good idea to offer a range of options to suit different needs.

Also, keep in mind that some people have food allergies or intolerances. It's important to clearly label your meals with all ingredients and highlight common allergens like nuts, dairy, or gluten.

By understanding macronutrients and micronutrients, you can create meals that not only satisfy hunger but also contribute to your customers' overall health and wellbeing. This knowledge can set your meal prep business apart and help your customers achieve their health goals, one delicious meal at a time.

Portion control

Portion control is like being a skilled artist – it's all about getting the right balance. In your meal prep business, mastering portion control can make a big difference in your customers' satisfaction and health. Let's dive into why it matters and how to do it well.

First off, why is portion control important? Well, it helps people eat the right amount of food for their needs. Eating too much can lead to weight gain, while eating too little might leave someone feeling hungry or missing out on important nutrients. Good portion control helps strike that perfect balance.

When you're planning your meals, think about using the "plate method" as a guide. Imagine dividing a plate into sections:

Half the plate should be filled with vegetables or fruits. These are packed with vitamins, minerals, and fiber, and they're generally low in calories.

One quarter of the plate should be protein. This could be meat, fish, eggs, or plant-based proteins like beans or tofu.

The last quarter should be grains or starchy vegetables. Think things like rice, pasta, or potatoes.

This method gives a good visual guide for creating balanced meals. But remember, the actual amount of food will vary depending on the person's needs. A big, active guy might need larger portions than a smaller, less active woman.

Now, let's talk about some practical ways to control portions in your meal prep business:

Use standard-sized containers: Having containers that are all the same size makes it easier to portion out meals consistently. You might have different sizes for different meal plans (like a smaller size for weight loss plans and a larger size for athletes).

Invest in good measuring tools: Kitchen scales, measuring cups, and scoops are your friends here. They help ensure you're putting the same amount of food in each container every time.

Create a portion guide for your team: Make a chart or guide that shows exactly how much of each ingredient should go into each meal. This helps keep things consistent, even if different people are preparing the meals.

Be mindful of calorie-dense foods: Things like oils, nuts, and cheese are healthy in small amounts but can add a lot of calories quickly. Use them sparingly and measure them carefully.

Consider offering different portion sizes: Some of your customers might want smaller portions for weight loss, while others might need larger portions for muscle gain. Having options can help you cater to different needs.

Don't forget about snacks: If you offer snacks as part of your meal prep service, portion these out too. A small container of nuts or sliced fruit can be a great addition to a meal plan.

Use visual cues: Sometimes it helps to think in terms of everyday objects. For example, a portion of meat should be about the size of a deck of cards, while a portion of cheese should be about the size of your thumb.

Remember, portion control isn't about restricting food – it's about providing the right amount. Your goal is to make sure your customers feel satisfied after their meals, not stuffed or still hungry.

It's also worth noting that portion sizes can vary depending on the specific diet plan. For example, a low-carb diet might have smaller portions of grains and larger portions of protein and vegetables. If you offer specialized meal plans, make sure your portion sizes align with the principles of that diet.

Lastly, be transparent about your portions. Let your customers know how big your portions are and what nutritional value they provide. This information can be really helpful for people who are tracking their food intake.

Mastering portion control takes practice, but it's an important skill for any meal prep business. It helps ensure your customers are getting the right amount of nutrients, supports their health goals, and can even help you manage your food costs better.

Dietary Preferences and Restrictions

Vegan, vegetarian, gluten-free, keto, etc.

In the world of meal prep, being able to cater to different dietary preferences and restrictions opens up your business to a wider range of customers and shows that you care about meeting everyone's needs. Let's break down some of the most common dietary preferences and restrictions you might encounter.

First up, let's talk about vegetarian and vegan diets. Vegetarians don't eat meat, while vegans avoid all animal products, including eggs and dairy. These diets are becoming more popular, so it's smart to have options for these customers. When creating vegetarian or vegan meals, focus on plant-based proteins like beans, lentils, tofu, and tempeh. You can make delicious meals like chickpea curry, lentil shepherd's pie, or stir-fry with tofu. Remember, vegan doesn't have to mean boring – there are tons of exciting plant-based ingredients out there to experiment with!

Next, we have gluten-free diets. Gluten is a protein found in wheat, barley, and rye. Some people avoid it due to celiac disease, while others find they feel better without it. For gluten-free meals, you'll need to skip traditional pasta, bread, and many sauces that contain wheat. Instead, use alternatives like rice, quinoa, or gluten-free pasta made from corn or rice. Be careful of hidden sources of gluten, like soy sauce or some spice mixes. Always check your ingredients carefully.

Keto is another popular diet. It's high in fat, moderate in protein, and very low in carbs. Keto meals might include things like grilled chicken with a creamy sauce and roasted low-carb vegetables, or a burger patty with avocado and a side salad (no bun, of course). When preparing keto meals, you'll need to be extra mindful of hidden carbs in sauces and seasonings.

Paleo is a diet based on foods that our ancient ancestors might have eaten. It includes meat, fish, vegetables, fruits, nuts, and seeds, but avoids grains, legumes, and dairy. A paleo meal might be grilled salmon with roasted sweet potatoes and a mix of vegetables.

Low-carb diets are similar to keto but not as strict. These meals focus on proteins and vegetables while limiting starchy foods. A low-carb meal could be a chicken breast with a large serving of roasted vegetables and a small portion of quinoa.

Some customers might follow specific eating patterns like intermittent fasting. While this doesn't change what they eat, it might affect when they want their meals delivered or how they want them packaged.

When catering to these different diets, it's important to understand the principles behind each one. This will help you create meals that truly fit the diet, not just technically meet the requirements. For example, a vegan meal should be satisfying and nutritionally complete, not just a regular meal with the meat removed.

It's also a good idea to offer customization options. Maybe a customer follows a mostly vegetarian diet but occasionally eats fish, or perhaps they're doing a low-carb diet but want to include small amounts of whole grains. Being flexible can help you meet more customers' needs.

Remember, these diets aren't just trends – for many people, they're important lifestyle choices or health necessities. By offering a range of options, you're not just expanding your customer base; you're helping people stick to their chosen way of eating, which can be a big relief for them.

Lastly, always be honest about what's in your meals. If something contains an ingredient that doesn't fit a certain diet, make sure that's clear. It's better to lose a sale than to lose a customer's trust. With careful planning and a bit of creativity, you can create delicious meals for all sorts of dietary preferences and restrictions!

Allergen management

Managing allergens in your meal prep business is super important – it's not just about making tasty food, it's about keeping your customers safe. Food allergies can be really serious, even life-threatening, so it's crucial to take them seriously. Let's talk about how to handle allergens in your kitchen.

First, let's go over the most common food allergens. In the United States, there are eight foods that account for about 90% of all food allergies:

- ◊ Milk
- ◊ Eggs
- ◊ Peanuts
- ◊ Tree nuts (like almonds, walnuts, and cashews)
- ◊ Fish
- ◊ Shellfish
- ◊ Soy
- ◊ Wheat

Some other common allergens include sesame, celery, and sulfites. It's a good idea to be aware of these too.

Now, how do you manage these allergens in your meal prep business? Here are some key steps:

Start with your ingredients. When you're buying ingredients, always check the labels carefully. Some allergens can hide in unexpected places. For example, soy sauce often contains wheat, and some spice mixes might contain peanut flour.

In your kitchen, store allergen-containing foods separately from other ingredients. This helps prevent accidental cross-contamination. You might use a separate shelf in your fridge or pantry for allergen-free ingredients.

When you're preparing meals, try to have designated areas for allergen-free cooking. If that's not possible, make sure to thoroughly clean all surfaces and utensils between preparing different meals. This is especially important for things like cutting boards and blenders, which can trap food particles.

Consider using color-coding in your kitchen. For example, you might use red cutting boards and utensils for meals containing allergens, and green for allergen-free meals. This visual system can help prevent mix-ups.

Train your staff thoroughly on allergen management. Everyone who works in your kitchen should understand the importance of avoiding cross-contamination and know how to handle allergen-free meal requests.

When it comes to packaging your meals, clear labeling is crucial. Every meal should be clearly labeled with all ingredients, with allergens highlighted or bolded. Don't forget about "may contain" warnings for foods that might have come into contact with allergens during processing.

It's also a good idea to have a system for customers to easily communicate their allergies to you. This might be a form on your website where they can list their allergies, or a clear process for noting allergies on orders.

Remember, even tiny amounts of an allergen can cause a reaction in some people. So if a customer asks for a meal without a certain ingredient, it's not enough to just leave it out – you need to make sure there's no cross-contamination at any stage of preparation.

If you're not sure whether a meal is safe for someone with a particular allergy, it's always better to say no than to risk their health. Be honest with your customers about what you can and can't guarantee.

Consider offering some completely allergen-free meals. For example, you might have a line of meals that are free from all of the top eight allergens. This can be a great option for customers with multiple allergies.

Lastly, stay informed about allergen regulations in your area. Rules about allergen labeling and management can vary, so make sure you're following all local guidelines.

By taking allergens seriously, you're not just protecting your customers – you're also building trust and showing that you care about their wellbeing. This can lead to loyal customers who appreciate your attention to detail and commitment to their safety.

Recipe Development

Sourcing ingredients

Finding the right ingredients for your meal prep business is like going on a treasure hunt. It's exciting, challenging, and when you find what you're looking for, it feels like striking gold! Let's talk about how to source the best ingredients for your meals.

First things first, you need to decide what kind of ingredients you want to use. Are you going for all organic? Local produce? Grass-fed meats? Your choices here will shape your menu and your brand, so think carefully about what matters most to you and your customers.

Once you know what you're looking for, it's time to start searching. A great place to start is local farmers' markets. Here, you can find fresh, seasonal produce and often meet the farmers who grew it. This is awesome for two reasons: you get super fresh ingredients, and you can tell your customers exactly where their food came from. People love knowing the story behind their meals!

For items you can't find at farmers' markets, look into local wholesalers. These are companies that sell ingredients in bulk to restaurants and food businesses. They often have a wide range of products and can be more cost-effective than buying from regular grocery stores.

Don't forget about specialty suppliers. If you're using unique ingredients or catering to specific diets, you might need to find suppliers who specialize in those items. For example, if you're making a lot of vegan meals, you might want to find a supplier who focuses on plant-based proteins.

When you're choosing suppliers, think about more than just price. Consider things like:

Quality: Are the ingredients consistently good?

Reliability: Can they deliver what you need, when you need it?

Flexibility: Can they handle changes in your orders?

Values: Do they align with your business values (like sustainability or supporting local farms)?

It's a good idea to have backup suppliers for your most important ingredients. This way, if one supplier can't deliver, you have another option.

Remember, building good relationships with your suppliers is super important. They're not just selling you ingredients – they're your partners in creating great meals. Take the time to get to know them, understand their business, and communicate clearly about your needs.

As your business grows, you might want to consider working directly with farms or producers. This can give you more control over the quality and type of ingredients you're getting. It might even allow you to have custom ingredients grown just for your business!

Don't be afraid to ask for samples before committing to a large order. This lets you test the quality and see how the ingredients work in your recipes.

Lastly, keep an eye on food trends and be open to trying new ingredients. Maybe there's a new type of grain that's becoming popular, or a vegetable that's not commonly used but could add something special to your meals. Being innovative with your ingredients can help set your meal prep business apart.

Remember, the ingredients you choose are the foundation of your meals. By sourcing high-quality, interesting ingredients, you're setting yourself up to create delicious, exciting meals that will keep your customers coming back for more. Happy ingredient hunting!

Standardizing recipes

Standardizing recipes in your meal prep business is like creating a blueprint for each dish. It's super important because it helps make sure every meal you send out is just as tasty as the last one. Let's dive into how to make your recipes consistent and reliable.

First off, why is standardizing recipes so important? Well, imagine if every time you ordered your favorite meal, it tasted different. Sometimes it might be too salty, other times not salty enough. That would be pretty disappointing, right? Standardizing your recipes helps avoid this problem. It means that no matter who's cooking in your kitchen, the meals will always taste the same.

So, how do you standardize a recipe? Let's break it down step by step.

Start by writing down every single ingredient in your recipe. And I mean every single one! Don't just say "spices" - list out exactly which spices and how much of each. Instead of "a pinch of salt," use a precise measurement like "1/4 teaspoon of salt."

Next, write out all the steps in order. Be super clear about what to do. Instead of saying "cook until done," say something like "cook for 15-20 minutes, until the internal temperature reaches 165°F (74°C)."

Now, here's a cool trick: make your recipes scalable. This means writing them in a way that makes it easy to make more or less of the dish. One way to do this is to list ingredients by weight rather than volume. So instead of "1 cup of chopped onions," you might say "150 grams of chopped onions." This makes it much easier to scale the recipe up or down.

Don't forget about equipment! List out what tools and equipment are needed for each recipe. This helps make sure everyone in the kitchen is using the same tools, which can affect how the food turns out.

Photos can be really helpful too. Take pictures of what the dish should look like at different stages of preparation. This gives your kitchen staff a visual guide to follow.

Once you've written out your standardized recipe, it's time to test it. Have different people in your kitchen make the recipe and see if they all get the same result. If not, you might need to make your instructions clearer or adjust some measurements.

Remember, standardizing recipes isn't just about the ingredients and steps. It's also about how the food is presented. Make sure to include instructions on how the meal should be plated or packaged. This helps ensure that every meal looks as good as it tastes.

It's a good idea to create a recipe book or database for your business. This could be a physical binder or a digital file that all your kitchen staff can access. Keep it updated with any changes or new recipes.

Standardized recipes are also super helpful for training new staff. When you have clear, detailed recipes, it's much easier to teach someone how to make your meals.

Don't forget about allergens and dietary restrictions. Make sure your standardized recipes clearly note any common allergens and suggest substitutions for different dietary needs.

Lastly, be open to improving your recipes over time. Maybe you'll find a way to make a dish taste even better, or a more efficient way to prepare it. When you make changes, make sure to update your standardized recipe right away.

Standardizing your recipes takes time and effort, but it's totally worth it. It helps ensure consistent quality, makes your kitchen run more smoothly, and gives your customers the reliable, delicious meals they're looking for. Plus, it makes your life easier in the long run. With standardized recipes, you can be confident that your meal prep business is putting out great food every single time.

Costing and pricing

Figuring out how much to charge for your meals is like solving a puzzle. You want to make enough money to keep your business running, but you also want your prices to be fair for your customers. Let's break down how to cost and price your meals in a way that makes sense for everyone.

First, let's talk about costing. This means figuring out how much it costs you to make each meal. To do this, you need to add up all the expenses that go into creating and delivering your meals. These expenses fall into two main categories: direct costs and indirect costs.

Direct costs are the things that directly go into making your meals. This includes:

Ingredients: Every bit of food that goes into the meal.

Packaging: The containers, labels, and bags you use to package the meals.

Labor: The time it takes your staff to prepare, cook, and package the meals.

To figure out your ingredient costs, use your standardized recipes. Add up the cost of each ingredient used in the recipe. Don't forget to account for any waste or trimmings.

For packaging, calculate the cost of all materials used for each meal, including containers, labels, and any additional packaging like bags or boxes.

Labor costs can be a bit trickier. You need to figure out how long it takes to prepare each meal and multiply that by your labor cost per hour. Don't forget to include time for cleaning up and packaging.

Indirect costs are expenses that aren't directly tied to making individual meals, but are necessary for running your business. These might include:

- Rent for your kitchen space

- Utilities like electricity and water

- Equipment costs

- Marketing expenses

- Administrative costs

To include these in your meal costs, you need to divide them up among all the meals you produce. One way to do this is to add a percentage to each meal's direct costs to cover these indirect expenses.

Once you've added up all these costs, you'll know how much it costs you to produce each meal. This is your break-even point - the minimum you need to charge just to cover your costs.

Now comes the tricky part: deciding how much to charge. You need to add a markup to your costs to make a profit. How much markup you add depends on a few things:

- Your target profit margin
- What your competitors are charging
- What your customers are willing to pay

A common approach is to use a food cost percentage. Many restaurants aim for food costs to be about 30% of the price they charge. So if a meal costs you $5 to make, you might charge around $16.67 for it ($5 divided by 0.3).

But remember, meal prep is different from restaurants. You might be able to have a lower food cost percentage because you're making meals in bulk and don't have the same overhead as a restaurant.

It's a good idea to research what other meal prep businesses in your area are charging. You don't want to be way more expensive than everyone else, but you also don't want to be so cheap that people question the quality of your food.

Consider offering different price points. Maybe you have a basic plan that's more affordable, and a premium plan with fancier ingredients that costs a bit more. This way, you can cater to different budgets.

Don't forget about special dietary needs. Meals that require special ingredients (like gluten-free or organic) might need to be priced higher to cover the extra costs.

Remember, it's okay to adjust your prices over time. As your costs change or as you learn more about what your customers want, you can tweak your pricing. Just be sure to communicate clearly with your customers about any price changes.

Lastly, think about the value you're providing beyond just the food. Are you saving your customers time? Helping them eat healthier? Make sure your pricing reflects the full value of your service.

CHAPTER 5
SOURCING INGREDIENTS

Finding Reliable Suppliers

The quality of your meal prep business hinges on the ingredients you use. Finding dependable suppliers who can consistently deliver high-quality produce, meats, and other essentials is crucial to your success.

Local vs. National Suppliers

Pros and cons

Choosing between local and national suppliers for your meal prep business is like picking teammates for a big game. Both have their strengths and weaknesses, and the right choice depends on what your business needs. Let's break down the good and not-so-good parts of each option.

Local Suppliers: The Hometown Heroes

Working with local suppliers is like having a friend who lives next door. They're close by, you can easily chat with them, and they understand what's happening in your neighborhood. Here's why local suppliers can be great:

Fresh as can be: Local suppliers often provide super fresh ingredients. Fruits and veggies might have been picked just yesterday, and that freshness can really make your meals stand out.

Supporting the community: When you buy from local suppliers, you're helping other businesses in your area grow. It's like being part of a team where everyone helps each other out.

Unique ingredients: Local suppliers might have special ingredients that you can't find anywhere else. Maybe there's a type of apple that only grows in your area, or a cheese made by a local farm. These unique touches can make your meals extra special.

Flexibility: Local suppliers are often more willing to work with you on things like order sizes or delivery times. If you suddenly need extra tomatoes for a big order, a local supplier might be able to help you out quickly.

Story to tell: People love knowing where their food comes from. When you use local suppliers, you can tell your customers exactly who grew their vegetables or raised their chickens. It's like giving each ingredient its own backstory.

But local suppliers aren't perfect. Here are some challenges you might face:

Higher prices: Sometimes, local ingredients can cost more than those from big national suppliers. This is because local suppliers often can't produce things in huge quantities, which can make their prices higher.

Limited selection: Depending on where you live, local suppliers might not be able to provide everything you need. For example, if you live in a cold area, you might not be able to get local tropical fruits.

Seasonal changes: Local produce changes with the seasons. This can be great for creating seasonal menus, but it also means you might need to change your recipes more often.

Inconsistent supply: Smaller local suppliers might sometimes run out of things you need, especially if bad weather affects their crops.

National Suppliers: The Big League Players

National suppliers are like the major league teams of the food world. They're big, they have a lot of resources, and they can usually provide whatever you need. Here's why national suppliers can be awesome:

Consistent supply: National suppliers usually have a steady supply of ingredients all year round. If you need tomatoes in winter, they've got you covered.

Lower prices: Because they deal in huge quantities, national suppliers can often offer lower prices than local ones.

Wide selection: National suppliers can usually provide almost any ingredient you might need, from common vegetables to exotic spices.

Standardized quality: Big suppliers often have strict quality control measures, so you know what you're getting will be consistent every time.

Efficient ordering: Many national suppliers have online ordering systems that make it easy to get what you need with just a few clicks.

But national suppliers have their downsides too:

Less personal service: With big national suppliers, you might not get the same personal attention that a local supplier would give you.

Longer supply chain: Food from national suppliers often travels long distances, which can affect freshness and increase the environmental impact.

Minimum order requirements: Some national suppliers have minimum order sizes that might be too large for a small or starting meal prep business.

Less flexibility: Big suppliers might not be as willing to accommodate special requests or last-minute changes.

Harder to trace: It can be more difficult to know exactly where your food is coming from with national suppliers, which might matter to some of your customers.

So, which should you choose? The truth is, many successful meal prep businesses use a mix of both. You might get your staple ingredients from a national supplier for consistency and cost-effectiveness, while sourcing special items or seasonal produce from local suppliers. This way, you get the best of both worlds – the reliability of national suppliers and the uniqueness of local ones.

Remember, your choice of suppliers is part of your business's story. Think about what matters most to you and your customers. Is it having the lowest prices possible? The freshest ingredients? Supporting local farms? Your answers to these questions will guide you towards the right mix of suppliers for your meal prep business.

Building Relationships with Suppliers

Negotiating contracts

Building good relationships with your suppliers is like making friends in a new neighborhood. It takes time, effort, and good communication, but it's totally worth it. Let's talk about how to build these relationships, starting with negotiating contracts.

Negotiating contracts with suppliers might sound scary, but it's really just about having a good conversation to make sure everyone's happy. Here's how to approach it:

Start with research: Before you talk to a supplier, know what you need and what's reasonable to ask for. Look into what other businesses similar to yours are getting. It's like doing your homework before a big test – the more you know, the better prepared you'll be.

Be clear about what you want: When you start talking to a supplier, be super clear about what you need. How much of each ingredient do you need? How often do you need deliveries? What quality standards are you looking for? The clearer you are, the easier it is for the supplier to understand if they can meet your needs.

Listen to the supplier: Remember, negotiation is a two-way street. Listen to what the supplier can offer and what challenges they might face. Maybe they can give you a better price if you order a little more, or maybe they can offer faster delivery if you're flexible on delivery days.

Think long-term: When you're negotiating, don't just think about what you need right now. Think about what you might need in the future as your business grows. It's like planting a tree – you want to choose a spot where it has room to grow.

Be fair: Remember, you want to build a relationship that lasts. If you push too hard for low prices, the supplier might not be able to give you good quality or reliable service. Aim for a deal that's fair for both sides.

Get it in writing: Once you've agreed on everything, make sure it's all written down in a contract. This protects both you and the supplier. It's like writing down the rules for a game – everyone knows what to expect.

Be open to renegotiation: As your business grows and changes, your needs might change too. Be open to talking with your suppliers about adjusting your agreements. Maybe you can get a better deal if you're ordering more, or maybe you need to change delivery schedules as you get busier.

Ensuring quality and consistency

Now, let's talk about making sure you're getting good quality ingredients consistently. This is super important for your meal prep business – your customers expect their meals to be delicious every single time.

Here are some ways to ensure quality and consistency:

Set clear standards: Tell your suppliers exactly what you expect. If you're ordering tomatoes, what size should they be? How ripe? What color? The more specific you are, the more likely you are to get what you want.

Do regular checks: When you get deliveries, check the quality of the ingredients. It's like being a food detective – look for any signs that things aren't up to your standards.

Give feedback: If something's not right, tell your supplier right away. Most suppliers want to do a good job and will appreciate knowing if there's a problem. It's like telling a friend if they have food stuck in their teeth – it might be a little awkward, but it's better for everyone in the long run.

Visit your suppliers: If possible, visit the farms or facilities where your food comes from. This helps you understand how things are grown or made, and it shows your suppliers that you care about quality.

Build personal relationships: Get to know the people you're working with. Learn their names, ask about their families, remember their birthdays. When you have a good personal relationship, people are more likely to go the extra mile for you.

Be a good customer: Pay your bills on time, be clear in your communication, and be understanding if small problems come up. If you're good to work with, suppliers will want to keep you happy.

Consider backup suppliers: It's good to have a backup plan in case your main supplier can't deliver what you need. It's like having a spare tire in your car – you hope you won't need it, but you're glad it's there if you do.

Keep records: Keep track of the quality of each delivery. This can help you spot trends over time and give you solid information if you need to discuss quality issues with a supplier.

Remember, building good relationships with suppliers takes time and effort, but it's a key part of running a successful meal prep business. When you have strong relationships with reliable suppliers, you can focus on creating amazing meals for your customers, knowing that you'll always have the high-quality ingredients you need.

Sustainable and Ethical Sourcing

Organic and non-GMO options

Sustainable and ethical sourcing is becoming more and more important in the food world. Let's talk about how you can make your meal prep business more sustainable and ethical, starting with organic and non-GMO options.

Organic food is grown without synthetic pesticides or fertilizers. It's like letting nature do its thing without adding any artificial helpers. Here's why you might want to consider organic ingredients:

Health: Some people believe organic food is healthier because it doesn't have residues from synthetic pesticides.

Environment: Organic farming practices are often better for the soil and local ecosystems. It's like being kind to the earth.

Taste: Some people think organic produce tastes better. It's like the difference between a homegrown tomato and one from a big supermarket.

But organic ingredients can be more expensive and sometimes harder to find in large quantities. You'll need to decide if the benefits are worth the extra cost for your business.

Non-GMO means the food hasn't been genetically modified. GMOs are plants or animals whose genes have been changed in a lab. Some people prefer non-GMO foods because:

Natural: They feel it's more natural to eat foods that haven't been genetically altered.

Environmental concerns: Some worry about the long-term effects of GMOs on the environment.

Personal beliefs: Some people just aren't comfortable with the idea of genetically modified food.

Like organic food, non-GMO ingredients can sometimes be more expensive or harder to find.

If you decide to use organic or non-GMO ingredients, make sure to let your customers know. Many people are willing to pay a bit more for these options. It's like offering a special edition of your meals.

Fair trade and local sourcing

Now let's talk about fair trade and local sourcing. These are ways to make sure the people who grow and produce your ingredients are treated fairly and to support your local community.

Fair trade is all about making sure farmers and workers in developing countries get a fair deal. When you buy fair trade ingredients, you're helping to:

Ensure fair wages: Fair trade farmers and workers get paid enough to support themselves and their families.

Improve working conditions: Fair trade standards include things like safe working environments and no child labor.

Support community development: Some of the money from fair trade goes back into the community for things like schools and healthcare.

Fair trade is most common for ingredients like coffee, chocolate, and bananas. Using fair trade ingredients in your meals is like giving your customers a chance to make the world a little bit better with every bite.

Local sourcing means getting your ingredients from nearby farms and producers. It's like being best friends with your neighbors. Here's why local sourcing can be great:

Freshness: Local food doesn't have to travel far, so it's often fresher.

Supporting the local economy: When you buy local, you're helping businesses in your community thrive.

Environmental benefits: Food that doesn't travel far uses less fuel for transportation, which is good for the environment.

Unique local flavors: You might find special local ingredients that can make your meals stand out.

Local sourcing can be a bit more work because you might need to deal with multiple small suppliers instead of one big one. But many customers love knowing their food comes from nearby.

When you're thinking about sustainable and ethical sourcing, here are some tips:

Start small: You don't have to change everything at once. Maybe start with one or two key ingredients and go from there.

Tell your story: Let your customers know about your sourcing choices. People love to hear the story behind their food.

Be transparent: If you can't source everything sustainably or ethically, be honest about it. Customers appreciate honesty.

Look for certifications: Things like USDA Organic, Fair Trade Certified, or local farm certifications can help you know you're making good choices.

Build relationships: Get to know the farmers and producers you're buying from. Understanding their work can help you make better decisions and tell better stories to your customers.

Consider the whole picture: Sometimes, local might be better than organic, or fair trade might be more important than non-GMO. Think about what matters most to you and your customers.

Be prepared for challenges: Sustainable and ethical sourcing can sometimes mean dealing with higher costs, seasonal availability, or supply challenges. But many businesses find it's worth it in the long run.

Remember, every step towards more sustainable and ethical sourcing is a good one. You don't have to be perfect – just keep trying to make good choices. Your customers will appreciate your efforts, and you'll be doing your part to make the food world a little bit better.

CHAPTER 6
MARKETING AND SALES

Building Your Brand

In the competitive world of meal prep, a strong brand can be the secret ingredient that sets you apart from the crowd. Your brand is more than just a logo or a catchy slogan; it's the personality of your business, the promise you make to your customers, and the experience you deliver with every meal.

Brand Identity

Logo and visual elements

Creating a brand identity for your meal prep business gives your company a face and personality. It's how people will recognize and remember you. Let's start with the logo and visual elements – these are the clothes your business wears to make a great first impression.

Your logo is the star of your visual identity. It's the symbol that will appear on your packaging, website, social media, and pretty much everywhere else. A good logo is simple, memorable, and tells people something about your business. For a meal prep company, you might want to include elements that suggest fresh food, health, or convenience.

When designing your logo, think about colors. Different colors can make people feel different things. Green often makes people think of health and freshness, while red can make them feel excited or hungry. Blue can make people feel calm and trustworthy. Pick colors that match the feeling you want your business to give.

The shape of your logo matters too. Round shapes can feel friendly and approachable, while sharp angles might look more modern and efficient. Think about what fits your business best.

Don't forget about the font you use for any words in your logo. A playful, curvy font might work for a fun, casual meal prep service, while a clean, simple font could be better for a more serious, health-focused brand.

Once you have your logo, you can create other visual elements that match it. This might include patterns, icons, or specific photo styles. These elements will help make all your materials look like they belong together.

Now, you might be thinking, "I'm not a designer! How can I create all this?" Don't worry – you don't have to do it all yourself. There are lots of ways to get help:

Freelance designers: Websites like Upwork or Fiverr let you hire designers for specific projects. You can look at their past work and choose someone whose style you like.

Design contests: Sites like 99designs let you describe what you want and then lots of designers submit ideas. You pick your favorite and work with that designer to finish it.

DIY tools: If you want to try designing yourself, tools like Canva or Adobe Spark make it easier to create professional-looking designs, even if you're not a pro.

Local design students: Art schools or design programs often have talented students looking for real-world projects. This can be a more affordable option.

Remember, your visual identity should reflect what makes your meal prep business special. Are you all about super healthy, organic meals? Your visuals might be clean and natural-looking. Is your thing gourmet meals for busy professionals? You might want a more sophisticated, upscale look.

Whatever you choose, make sure it's consistent across everything you do. Your packaging, website, social media, and even your delivery vehicles (if you have them) should all look like they're part of the same family. This consistency helps build trust and makes your brand more memorable.

Brand voice and messaging

Now that we've talked about how your brand looks, let's talk about how it sounds. Your brand voice is like your business's personality – it's how you talk to your customers in all your communications.

Your brand voice should match your visual identity and your overall business goals. Are you casual and friendly, or more formal and professional? Do you use humor, or keep things serious? Think about your ideal customer and how they would want to be spoken to.

For a meal prep business, you might want a voice that's:

Encouraging: You're helping people eat better and live healthier lives.

Knowledgeable: You know a lot about nutrition and good food.

Practical: You understand people's busy lives and how your service helps.

Your messaging is what you actually say using your brand voice. This includes things like:

Your slogan or tagline: A short phrase that sums up what you're all about.

Your mission statement: A sentence or two explaining why your business exists.

Your key selling points: The main reasons why people should choose your meal prep service.

When creating your messaging, think about what makes your meal prep business different from others. Maybe you use all organic ingredients, or you have a chef with fancy restaurant experience. Whatever it is, make sure to highlight it in your messaging.

It's also important to be consistent with your messaging across all platforms. Whether someone's reading your website, your social media, or the label on your meal containers, they should get the same idea about who you are and what you offer.

Remember, your brand voice and messaging can evolve over time as your business grows and changes. Just make sure any changes are thoughtful and gradual so you don't confuse your customers.

Online Presence

Website development

In today's digital world, having a good website is like having a welcoming storefront for your meal prep business. It's often the first place potential customers will go to learn about you, so it needs to make a great impression.

Your website should be:

Easy to use: People should be able to find what they're looking for quickly and easily.

Mobile-friendly: Lots of people browse on their phones, so your site needs to look good on small screens.

Fast to load: If your site is slow, people might give up and go somewhere else.

Secure: If you're taking orders or payments on your site, it needs to be extra secure.

Here's what your meal prep business website might include:
- A clear explanation of what you offer
- Your menu, with photos of your meals
- Nutritional information for your meals
- Information about your ingredients and cooking methods
- How to order
- Pricing and subscription options
- About us page telling your business's story
- Contact information
- FAQ section

You might also want to include features like:
- Online ordering system
- Customer account pages where people can manage their subscriptions
- Blog with recipes or nutrition tips
- Customer reviews or testimonials

When it comes to actually building your website, you have a few options:

Website builders: Tools like Wix, Squarespace, or Shopify make it easy to build a professional-looking site without knowing how to code. They offer templates you can customize to fit your brand.

Hire a web developer: If you want something more custom or complex, you might want to hire a professional. You can find freelance web developers on sites like Upwork or through local tech meetups.

WordPress: This is a popular option that's somewhere in between. You can use pre-made themes and plugins, but it offers more flexibility than simple website builders. You might need some technical help to set it up, though.

Whatever option you choose, make sure your website reflects your brand identity. Use your logo, colors, and brand voice consistently throughout the site.

Don't forget about search engine optimization (SEO). This means using the right keywords and structuring your site in a way that helps it show up in search results when people are looking for meal prep services in your area.

Lastly, remember that your website is never really "finished." Plan to update it regularly with new menu items, blog posts, or customer testimonials to keep it fresh and engaging.

Social media strategy

Social media is like a bustling marketplace where you can connect with your customers, show off your meals, and attract new business. For a meal prep company, it's an especially powerful tool because food is so visual and shareable.

Here's how to create a social media strategy for your meal prep business:

Choose the right platforms: You don't need to be on every social media site. Focus on the ones where your target customers spend time. For meal prep, Instagram and Facebook are often good choices because they're great for sharing food photos.

Post consistently: Decide how often you can realistically post and stick to that schedule. It's better to post high-quality content less often than to post low-quality content every day.

Share a mix of content: Don't just post ads for your service. Share things like:

- Beautiful photos of your meals
- Behind-the-scenes glimpses of your kitchen
- Tips for healthy eating
- Customer success stories
- Polls or questions to engage your followers

Use hashtags: These help people find your content. Use a mix of popular hashtags (#mealprep, #healthyeating) and more specific ones (#NYCmealprep, #glutenfreemeals).

Engage with your followers: Respond to comments, answer questions, and like and comment on other people's posts. Social media is a two-way conversation.

Consider influencer partnerships: Working with local food bloggers or fitness influencers can help you reach new audiences.

Use social media advertising: Platforms like Facebook and Instagram offer powerful targeting tools to help you reach potential customers in your area.

Track your results: Use the analytics tools provided by each platform to see what kinds of posts perform best and adjust your strategy accordingly.

Remember, social media is about building relationships, not just selling. Use it to show the personality behind your brand and to provide value to your followers beyond just promoting your meals.

Sales Channels

Direct-to-consumer (DTC)

Selling directly to consumers is like having your own little store, but without the physical storefront. It's a great way to build strong relationships with your customers and keep more of the profit for yourself.

For a meal prep business, DTC often means taking orders through your website or app and delivering meals directly to customers' homes or offices.
Here's how to make it work:

Make ordering easy: Your website or app should make it simple for people to choose their meals, set up recurring orders, and pay securely.

Offer flexible options: Some customers might want a full week of meals, while others just want a few. Offer different package sizes to suit different needs.

Provide great customer service: Be responsive to questions and concerns. Consider offering a satisfaction guarantee to build trust.

Get your delivery system right: Whether you're delivering yourself or using a service, make sure meals arrive on time and in good condition. Consider using eco-friendly packaging to appeal to environmentally conscious customers.

Collect and use customer data: With DTC, you can learn a lot about your customers' preferences. Use this information to improve your menu and target your marketing.

Partnerships with gyms, offices, and health clubs

Partnering with local businesses is like having a team of cheerleaders promoting your meals. Gyms, offices, and health clubs are full of potential customers who care about health and convenience.

Here's how to make these partnerships work:

Offer special deals: Give members of partner businesses a discount on their first order or a free meal to try.

Provide sample meals: Let people taste your food at events or in the partner's location.

Create co-branded marketing: Work with your partners to create flyers or social media posts that you both share.

Offer meal plans tailored to the partner's audience: For a gym, you might create a high-protein plan for bodybuilders. For an office, you might focus on easy lunch options.

Consider on-site delivery: If a large office orders enough meals, you could do a weekly group delivery to make it extra convenient for employees.

Remember, these partnerships should benefit both sides. Think about how you can add value for your partners, not just how they can help you.

Online marketplaces

Online marketplaces are like digital food courts where customers can browse meals from different prep services. Being on these platforms can help you reach customers who might not find you otherwise.

Popular marketplaces for meal prep businesses include:

- UberEats
- DoorDash
- GrubHub
- Postmates

Here's how to make the most of online marketplaces:

Choose the right platforms: Research which ones are popular in your area and fit your business model.

Optimize your listing: Use great photos and clear descriptions to make your meals stand out.

Price strategically: Remember that marketplaces take a cut of each sale, so factor that into your pricing.

Encourage reviews: Positive reviews can boost your visibility on the platform.

Use promotions wisely: Many marketplaces let you offer deals to attract new customers. Use these strategically to boost orders during slow times.

Be prepared for volume: If you're on a popular platform, you might get a lot of orders at once. Make sure you can handle the volume without sacrificing quality.

While marketplaces can be a great way to reach new customers, remember that they also take a significant cut of each sale. It's usually best to use them as part of a broader sales strategy, not as your only sales channel.

CHAPTER 7
OPERATIONS AND LOGISTICS

Order Management

Efficient order management is the backbone of a successful meal prep business. It's the intricate system that ensures your culinary creations make their way from your kitchen to your customers' tables, fresh and on time.

Order Processing Systems

Online ordering platforms

Setting up an efficient order processing system for your meal prep business acts as the backbone of your operations. It streamlines the process of taking orders, managing customer preferences, and ensuring accurate meal delivery. Let's dive into the world of online ordering platforms.

An online ordering platform serves as a digital interface between your business and your customers. It allows customers to browse your menu, select their desired meals, and complete their purchases, all from the comfort of their own devices. This convenience factor can significantly boost your sales and customer satisfaction.

When selecting an online ordering platform for your meal prep business, prioritize user-friendliness. The platform should work seamlessly on both desktop computers and mobile devices. It should present your menu in an attractive, easy-to-navigate format, allowing customers to quickly find and select their preferred meals.

Several popular online ordering platforms cater to meal prep businesses. Shopify stands out as a versatile e-commerce platform that can be customized to suit your specific needs. It offers a user-friendly interface and a wide range of features to enhance your customers' ordering experience.

For those using WordPress as their website platform, WooCommerce serves as an excellent plugin that can transform your site into a fully functional online store. It integrates seamlessly with WordPress and offers numerous extensions to tailor your ordering system.

Square, known primarily for its payment processing services, also provides robust online ordering tools. These work particularly well for food-based businesses and can integrate with other Square services you might use, such as point-of-sale systems.

ChowNow specializes in online ordering for food businesses. It offers features specifically designed for recurring orders, making it an excellent choice for meal prep services that focus on subscription-based models.

When setting up your online ordering system, ensure you provide comprehensive information about each meal. Include detailed descriptions, a full list of ingredients, and nutritional information. High-quality photos of your meals can significantly influence customers' decisions and increase sales.

Your ordering system should also accommodate any customization options you offer. This might include the ability to swap side dishes, choose between different protein options, or adjust portion sizes. A flexible system that can handle these variations will enhance customer satisfaction and set your business apart from competitors.

If the technical aspects of setting up an online ordering platform seem daunting, don't hesitate to seek professional help. Freelance developers on platforms like Upwork or Fiverr can assist in setting up and customizing your online ordering system. When hiring, look for developers with experience in food-related e-commerce to ensure they understand the unique needs of a meal prep business.

Your online ordering platform often serves as the first point of contact between your business and potential customers. Ensure it reflects your brand identity and provides an exceptional user experience. A smooth, intuitive ordering process can turn first-time buyers into loyal, long-term customers of your meal prep service.

Subscription models

Subscription models in the meal prep industry create a loyal customer base and provide a steady, predictable income stream. They allow customers to sign up for regular meal deliveries, typically on a weekly or monthly basis.

Implementing a subscription model offers numerous benefits for your meal prep business. It provides a consistent revenue stream, allowing for better financial planning and inventory management. Additionally, it helps build customer loyalty, as subscribers often stick with a service they enjoy for extended periods.

Consider offering various subscription options to cater to different customer needs:

Weekly plans allow customers to choose a set number of meals to receive each week. They might select new meals each week or opt for a repeating order of their favorites.

Monthly plans involve customers committing to a full month of meals at a time. This approach can improve your cash flow and allow for more efficient long-term planning.

Flexible plans give customers the freedom to choose a certain number of meals per month but schedule deliveries according to their preferences. This option caters to customers with varying schedules or those who don't want meals every single week.

When designing your subscription model, think about offering different plans to suit various lifestyles and dietary needs. For instance, you could create:

- An individual plan providing lunch and dinner options for each day
- A family plan with larger portions or kid-friendly meals
- Specialized plans catering to specific diets such as keto, vegetarian, or gluten-free

Ensure your online ordering system can handle subscriptions efficiently. Customers should be able to easily manage their subscriptions, including pausing for vacations, changing meal selections, or updating delivery information. A user-friendly subscription management system can significantly reduce customer service inquiries and improve overall satisfaction.

Consider offering incentives to encourage customers to subscribe. This could include a discount compared to ordering meals individually, access to exclusive menu items, or priority delivery slots. These perks can help convert one-time buyers into long-term subscribers.

In a subscription-based model, customer retention becomes crucial. Keep your subscribers engaged and satisfied by:

- Maintaining consistent quality across all meals

- Offering sufficient variety to prevent menu fatigue

- Providing exceptional customer service

- Sending occasional surprises or bonuses to show appreciation for their loyalty

A well-executed subscription model can provide a solid foundation for your meal prep business, creating a reliable customer base and steady income. It allows you to focus on perfecting your meals and growing your business, rather than constantly chasing new one-time orders.

Production Scheduling

Batch cooking

Batch cooking forms the cornerstone of efficient meal prep operations. This method involves preparing large quantities of food at once, rather than making individual meals separately. It significantly boosts productivity and ensures consistency across your meals.

In batch cooking, instead of preparing one serving at a time, you might cook 50 or 100 servings simultaneously. For example, you'd grill a large quantity of chicken breasts at once, chop vegetables in bulk, or prepare a big batch of sauce that can be used across multiple meal types.

This approach offers several advantages:

Time efficiency: Performing tasks in bulk generally proves faster than repeating the same task multiple times for individual meals.

Consistency: Large-batch preparation tends to yield more consistent results, ensuring that each portion of a particular dish tastes the same.

Cost-effectiveness: Buying ingredients in larger quantities often results in lower per-unit costs, improving your profit margins.

To implement batch cooking effectively in your meal prep business, careful planning becomes essential:

Create a detailed production schedule. Designate specific days for different tasks. For instance, Mondays could be dedicated to cooking all proteins, Tuesdays for vegetable prep, and so on.

Invest in appropriate equipment. Large-capacity cooking vessels, expansive baking sheets, and industrial-sized food processors can greatly facilitate batch cooking.

Develop a system for tracking batches. You might use color-coded containers or detailed labeling to organize and identify different batches easily.

Consider food safety when cooling and storing large batches. Rapid cooling is crucial to prevent bacterial growth. Invest in blast chillers or ice baths to cool food quickly and safely.

Adjust your ingredient sourcing to accommodate batch cooking. You'll need to purchase larger quantities, so ensure your suppliers can meet these increased demands.

Remember, batch cooking doesn't mean every meal must be identical. Create variety by using the same base ingredients in different combinations. For example, grilled chicken could feature in a salad, a wrap, or a grain bowl, providing diverse meal options from a single batch-cooked ingredient.

Mastering batch cooking requires practice. Begin with smaller batches and gradually increase quantities as you become more comfortable with the process. With time and experience, you'll perfect the art of batch cooking, enabling your meal prep business to produce delicious, consistent meals efficiently and profitably.

Inventory management

Effective inventory management serves as the backbone of a successful meal prep business. It enables you to track ingredient levels, predict future needs, and prevent costly shortages or overstock situations. Proper inventory management ensures smooth operations and helps maintain profitability.

To establish a robust inventory management system:

Maintain a comprehensive list of all ingredients. This should encompass not only main components like meats and vegetables but also spices, oils, and other items used regularly in your recipes.

Monitor ingredient usage closely. Track how quickly you go through each item to accurately predict future needs and optimize ordering.

Establish par levels for each ingredient. A par level represents the minimum quantity of an item you aim to have on hand at all times. When stock drops below this threshold, it signals the need to reorder.

Implement the "first in, first out" (FIFO) method. This approach involves using older ingredients before newer ones to minimize waste and ensure freshness.

Conduct regular physical inventory checks. Performing actual counts of your ingredients helps identify any discrepancies and prevents unexpected shortages.

Consider adopting inventory management software. These tools can streamline tracking and improve accuracy. Options tailored for food businesses include MarketMan, Orderly, and SimpleOrder.

Optimize your storage setup. Ensure you have adequate space to store ingredients properly, including sufficient refrigeration and dry storage areas.

Pay close attention to expiration dates. Use ingredients before they spoil to minimize waste and maintain meal quality.

Align your menu planning with your inventory. Feature ingredients that need to be used soon in upcoming meals to reduce waste.

Cultivate strong relationships with your suppliers. Good communication can help you quickly obtain ingredients when running low or facing unexpected demand.

Remember, effective inventory management involves striking a balance. While having enough ingredients on hand is crucial, overstocking can lead to waste and tie up capital in unused inventory.

By mastering inventory management, you'll enhance the efficiency and profitability of your meal prep business. You'll reduce food waste, minimize the stress of potential ingredient shortages, and free up more time to focus on creating delicious, high-quality meals for your customers.

Delivery and Distribution

In-house delivery vs. third-party services

The final step in your meal prep business involves getting your carefully prepared meals into your customers' hands. You have two primary options for this crucial task: managing deliveries in-house or partnering with third-party delivery services. Each approach has its own set of advantages and challenges.

In-house delivery puts you in complete control of the process. Here's what it entails:

Advantages:

- Full control over the delivery process
- Ability to maintain brand standards throughout the customer experience
- Opportunity for delivery staff to build relationships with regular customers
- Retention of all delivery fees

Challenges:

- Requires significant investment in vehicles, insurance, and staff
- Necessitates management of routing and logistics
- Can be difficult to scale quickly if business grows rapidly

To implement in-house delivery successfully, you'll need:

- Reliable delivery vehicles
- A team of trained drivers
- Appropriate insurance coverage for deliveries
- A system for efficient routing and delivery tracking

Third-party delivery services specialize in food delivery. Popular options include DoorDash, Uber Eats, and Grubhub. Here's what using these services involves:

Advantages:

- No need to invest in vehicles or hire drivers
- Access to the service's existing customer base, potentially reaching new customers
- Handling of all delivery logistics by the service

Challenges:

- Services take a significant percentage of each sale, impacting your profit margins
- Less control over the delivery process and customer experience
- Your meals may be delivered alongside orders from other restaurants, potentially affecting your brand image

To use third-party services effectively:

- Ensure your packaging can withstand the rigors of the delivery process
- Clearly communicate any special handling instructions for your meals

- Closely monitor customer feedback to identify and address any delivery-related issues

Many successful meal prep businesses employ a hybrid approach. They might handle deliveries for their regular subscription customers in-house while using third-party services for one-off orders or to reach new customers in different areas.

When deciding on your delivery strategy, consider:

- Your available budget
- The size of your delivery area
- Your anticipated daily delivery volume
- The level of control you desire over the delivery process
- Your plans for future growth

Remember, delivery often represents the final interaction your customers have with your business for each order. Whether you opt for in-house delivery or a third-party service, ensure it upholds your brand standards and leaves customers satisfied and eager to order again.

Packaging for freshness and safety

Packaging plays a crucial role in your meal prep business, serving multiple important functions. It protects your meals, maintains freshness, ensures food safety, and represents your brand to customers. Selecting the right packaging can significantly impact customer satisfaction and the success of your business.

When choosing packaging, consider the following factors:

Material: Your packaging must be food-safe and suitable for refrigeration or freezing. Common options include:

Plastic containers: Durable and often microwaveable, but may raise environmental concerns.

Glass containers: Reusable and microwaveable, but heavier and more expensive.

Compostable containers: Environmentally friendly, but potentially less durable for extended storage.

Size and shape: Containers should accommodate your portion sizes appropriately. Consider having different sizes for various meal types, such as salads versus hot entrees.

Sealing: A secure seal proves crucial for maintaining freshness and preventing spills during delivery. Look for containers with reliable, leak-proof lids.

Compartments: For meals with multiple components, containers with separate compartments can prevent foods from mixing and help maintain proper textures.

Temperature control: If delivering hot meals, you may need insulated packaging to maintain warmth. For cold items, consider including ice packs to ensure food safety.

Labeling: Your packaging should feature clear labels with:

- Meal name
- Complete ingredient list
- Nutritional information
- Heating instructions
- Use-by date
- Your company name and contact information

Branding: Utilize your packaging as a branding opportunity. Incorporate your logo and brand colors to make your meals instantly recognizable.

Eco-friendliness: Many customers appreciate environmentally conscious packaging. Consider options like recyclable or biodegradable materials to appeal to this growing consumer preference.

To ensure food safety, your packaging must:

- Maintain appropriate temperatures (hot foods above 140°F or 60°C, cold foods below 40°F or 4°C)
- Protect food from potential contamination
- Remain clean and sanitary throughout the delivery process

Your packaging contributes significantly to the overall customer experience. Attractive, convenient packaging can enhance meal enjoyment and reinforce positive associations with your brand.

To find the ideal packaging solution for your business:

- Request samples from various suppliers for testing
- Solicit feedback from your customers on packaging preferences
- Research packaging used by successful meal prep businesses in other markets

If you need assistance with packaging design, consider hiring freelance packaging designers through platforms like 99designs or Behance. These professionals can help create packaging that balances functionality with visual appeal.

Investing in high-quality packaging that keeps your meals fresh, safe, and visually appealing can yield substantial returns in customer satisfaction and brand loyalty for your meal prep business.

CHAPTER 8
CUSTOMER SERVICE AND RETENTION

Building Customer Relationships

In the meal prep business, your success hinges not just on the quality of your food, but on the strength of your customer relationships. Cultivating a loyal customer base is essential for sustainable growth and long-term success.

Customer Feedback

Surveys and reviews

Customer feedback serves as the lifeblood of any successful meal prep business. It provides invaluable insights into what your customers love, what they dislike, and what they wish you'd offer. By actively seeking and analyzing customer feedback, you can continuously improve your service and stay ahead of the competition.

Surveys stand out as an effective tool for gathering structured feedback from your customers. They allow you to ask specific questions about various aspects of your service, from meal quality to delivery experience. When creating surveys, keep them short and focused. Long surveys can deter customers from completing them, resulting in lower response rates.

Consider using a mix of question types in your surveys. Multiple-choice questions make it easy for customers to respond quickly, while open-ended questions allow them to provide more detailed feedback. You might ask questions such as:

"How would you rate the taste of your meals on a scale of 1 to 5?"

"Which meal was your favorite this week and why?"

"How satisfied are you with our delivery service?"

"What new meal options would you like to see on our menu?"

Timing matters when sending out surveys. You could send a quick satisfaction survey immediately after delivery, or a more comprehensive survey at the end of each week or month. Experiment with different timings to see when you get the best response rates.

Reviews, on the other hand, offer more spontaneous feedback from customers. They can be posted on your website, social media pages, or third-party review sites. While you have less control over the content of reviews compared to surveys, they often provide authentic, unfiltered opinions that can be incredibly valuable.

Encourage customers to leave reviews by making the process as easy as possible. Include links to review sites in your follow-up emails or on your packaging. You could even offer small incentives, like a discount on their next order, for customers who leave honest reviews.

When you receive reviews, good or bad, always respond. Thank customers for positive reviews and address any issues mentioned in negative ones. This shows that you value customer feedback and are committed to improving your service.

To make the most of the feedback you receive through surveys and reviews:

Analyze the data regularly. Look for patterns and trends in the responses. Are there certain meals that consistently get high ratings? Are there common complaints about delivery times or packaging?

Share the feedback with your team. Make sure everyone, from your chefs to your delivery drivers, understands what customers are saying about your service.

Use positive feedback in your marketing. With permission, you can use glowing reviews as testimonials on your website or social media.

Act on the feedback you receive. If multiple customers suggest a new meal idea, consider adding it to your menu. If there are frequent complaints about a particular aspect of your service, prioritize fixing it.

Implementing feedback

Collecting customer feedback is only half the battle. The real value comes from implementing that feedback to improve your meal prep business. This process involves carefully analyzing the feedback you've received, prioritizing changes, and effectively communicating these improvements to your customers.

Start by categorizing the feedback you receive. You might group it into areas such as meal quality, variety, portion sizes, delivery service, packaging, and customer support. This organization helps you identify which areas of your business are performing well and which need improvement.

Next, prioritize the changes you want to make. Consider factors such as:

- How frequently a particular issue is mentioned
- The potential impact of addressing the issue
- The resources required to implement the change
- How the change aligns with your overall business goals

For example, if many customers mention that they'd like more vegetarian options, and this aligns with your goal of catering to diverse dietary needs, you might prioritize developing new vegetarian meals. On the other hand, if only one customer mentions wanting gold-plated cutlery with their meals, that's probably not a change you need to prioritize.

Once you've decided on the changes you want to make, create an action plan. This should outline what needs to be done, who's responsible for doing it, and when it should be completed. Be realistic about timelines – some changes, like adjusting portion sizes, might be quick to implement, while others, like overhauling your entire menu, will take more time.

As you implement changes based on customer feedback, it's crucial to monitor their impact. Did adding more vegetarian options lead to an increase in orders? Did changing your packaging reduce complaints about food temperature? Continuously assess the effects of your changes to ensure they're having the desired impact.

Don't forget to close the feedback loop by informing your customers about the changes you've made. This shows that you value their input and are committed to improving their experience. You could do this through email newsletters, social media posts, or even personalized messages to customers who provided specific feedback.

For example, you might send an email saying, "You spoke, and we listened! Based on your feedback, we've added five new vegetarian options to our menu. We hope you'll try them and let us know what you think."

Implementing customer feedback effectively can lead to significant improvements in customer satisfaction and loyalty. It shows your customers that you care about their opinions and are willing to adapt to meet their needs. This responsiveness can set you apart from competitors and help build a strong, loyal customer base for your meal prep business.

Loyalty Programs

Discounts and rewards

Loyalty programs can significantly boost customer retention and increase the lifetime value of each customer for your meal prep business. By offering discounts and rewards, you incentivize customers to continue using your service and potentially increase their order frequency or size.

When designing a discount structure for your loyalty program, consider offering both immediate and long-term benefits. Immediate discounts give customers a reason to sign up right away, while long-term rewards encourage ongoing engagement with your service.

Here are some discount ideas you might consider:

Sign-up bonus: Offer a discount on the first order for new customers who join your loyalty program. This could be a percentage off their total order or a free meal with their first purchase.

Volume discounts: Reward customers who order larger quantities. For example, you could offer a 10% discount when ordering 10 or more meals per week.

Subscription discounts: If you offer a subscription service, provide a discount for customers who commit to longer subscription periods. A customer signing up for a 3-month subscription might get a bigger discount than someone on a month-to-month plan.

Milestone rewards: Offer special discounts when customers reach certain milestones. This could be their 10th order, their 6-month anniversary with your service, or when they've spent a certain amount in total.

Seasonal promotions: Create special discounts tied to seasons or holidays. A "New Year, New You" promotion in January or a "Summer Slim-Down" deal could attract customers looking to eat healthier during these times.

In addition to discounts, consider offering other types of rewards:

Free meals: After a certain number of orders, customers could earn a free meal of their choice.

Exclusive menu items: Give loyal customers early access to new menu items or special dishes not available to other customers.

Customization options: Allow loyal customers to make more extensive customizations to their meals at no extra charge.

Priority delivery: Offer preferred delivery time slots to your most loyal customers.

Branded merchandise: After reaching high loyalty tiers, customers could earn branded items like water bottles or meal prep containers.

When implementing your loyalty program, make sure it's easy for customers to understand and track their progress. A points-based system can work well, where customers earn points for each dollar spent or meal ordered. These points can then be redeemed for discounts or rewards.

Use your online ordering platform or a dedicated loyalty program app to help customers keep track of their rewards. Send regular updates on their point balances or when they're close to earning a new reward to keep them engaged.

Referral programs

Referral programs can be a powerful tool for growing your meal prep business. They turn your satisfied customers into brand ambassadors, helping you acquire new customers at a lower cost than traditional marketing methods.

The key to a successful referral program is to make it beneficial for both the referrer and the new customer. Here's how you might structure a referral program:

Offer a reward to the referring customer: This could be a discount on their next order, bonus loyalty points, or a free meal. The reward should be substantial enough to motivate customers to make referrals, but not so large that it eats into your profits.

Provide an incentive for the new customer: Give the referred friend a discount on their first order. This makes them more likely to try your service and potentially become a regular customer.

Make it easy to refer: Provide customers with a unique referral code or link that they can easily share with friends and family. This could be included in order confirmation emails, on your website, or in your mobile app.

Track referrals accurately: Use software that can track referrals and automatically apply rewards. This ensures that customers get credit for their referrals and receive their rewards promptly.

Promote your referral program: Make sure your customers know about the program. Mention it in your emails, on your website, and on social media. You could even include information about the referral program with each meal delivery.

Consider tiered rewards: Offer increasing rewards for customers who make multiple successful referrals. This encourages your most enthusiastic customers to continue spreading the word about your service.

Here's an example of how a referral program might work:

"Refer a friend to [**Your Meal Prep Business**], and you'll both win! When your friend places their first order using your unique referral code, they'll get $20 off their order. Once their order is delivered, you'll receive a $20 credit on your account. The more friends you refer, the more you save!"

A well-designed loyalty program, complete with attractive discounts, meaningful rewards, and an easy-to-use referral system, can significantly boost customer retention and acquisition for your meal prep business. It encourages customers to order more frequently, try new menu items, and share their positive experiences with others, all of which contribute to the growth and success of your business.

Handling Complaints and Issues

Effective communication

In the meal prep business, as in any customer-focused industry, complaints and issues will inevitably arise. How you handle these situations can make the difference between losing a customer and turning them into a loyal advocate for your brand. Effective communication plays a crucial role in resolving issues and maintaining customer satisfaction.

When a customer reaches out with a complaint, the first step is to listen actively and empathetically. Allow the customer to express their concerns fully without interruption. This not only helps you gather all the necessary information but also shows the customer that you value their input and take their concerns seriously.

Respond promptly to all complaints and inquiries. In today's fast-paced world, customers expect quick responses. Aim to acknowledge receipt of their complaint within a few hours, even if you can't provide a full resolution immediately. This initial response should thank the customer for their feedback and assure them that you're looking into the issue.

Use a friendly and professional tone in all your communications. Even if the customer is upset or angry, maintain a calm and courteous demeanor. This can help de-escalate tense situations and make the customer more receptive to your proposed solutions.

Be clear and specific in your communication. Avoid vague promises or technical jargon that the customer might not understand. Instead, explain clearly what went wrong (if you know), what you're going to do to fix it, and when the customer can expect a resolution.

Take responsibility for the issue, even if it wasn't directly your fault. Avoid making excuses or shifting blame. A simple "I apologize for the inconvenience this has caused you" can go a long way in diffusing a tense situation.

Offer solutions, not just apologies. While apologizing is important, customers want to know how you're going to make things right. Depending on the situation, this might involve replacing a meal, offering a refund, or providing a credit for future orders.

Follow up after the issue has been resolved. Check in with the customer to ensure they're satisfied with the outcome and to see if there's anything else you can do to improve their experience. This extra step shows that you care about their satisfaction beyond just resolving the immediate issue.

Use complaints as an opportunity to gather feedback and improve your service. Ask customers what you could have done differently to prevent the issue from occurring in the first place. Their insights can help you identify areas for improvement in your business processes.

Train your entire team in effective communication and complaint handling. Everyone who interacts with customers should be equipped to handle issues professionally and consistently. This might involve role-playing exercises or regular training sessions on customer service best practices.

Consider implementing a customer service platform or CRM system to help track and manage customer interactions. This can ensure that no complaints fall through the cracks and that you have a record of all communications with each customer.

Problem resolution strategies

Having a systematic approach to problem resolution can help you handle customer issues more effectively and consistently. Here are some strategies to consider:

Develop a clear escalation process: Not all issues can be resolved by the first person who receives the complaint. Have a clear process for when and how to escalate more complex or serious issues to management. This ensures that customers with significant problems receive the attention they need while allowing your front-line staff to handle routine issues efficiently.

Create a knowledge base of common issues and solutions: Document the problems that come up frequently and the most effective ways to resolve them. This resource can help your team respond to issues more quickly and consistently.

Empower your team to make decisions: Give your customer service representatives the authority to offer certain solutions without having to consult a manager for every issue. This might include the ability to offer refunds up to a certain amount or to send replacement meals without approval. This can lead to faster resolution times and increased customer satisfaction.

Use a tiered approach to compensation: Not all issues warrant the same level of compensation. Develop guidelines for what to offer based on the severity of the problem. For minor issues, a small discount on a future order might suffice. For more serious problems, you might need to offer a full refund and additional compensation.

Implement a service recovery paradox: This concept suggests that customers who have a problem that's resolved quickly and effectively often become more loyal than customers who never had a problem at all. With this in mind, view each complaint as an opportunity to strengthen your relationship with the customer.

Analyze patterns in complaints: Regularly review the issues that customers report to identify any recurring problems. This can help you address systemic issues in your operations and prevent future complaints.

Offer multiple channels for customers to reach you: Some customers prefer to call, others to email, and some might want to use social media or chat. By offering various ways for customers to contact you, you make it easier for them to report issues and for you to resolve them quickly.

Set and communicate clear expectations: Be upfront about your delivery times, meal options, and any limitations of your service. When customers have realistic expectations, they're less likely to be disappointed.

Use customer feedback to improve your service: After resolving an issue, ask the customer for suggestions on how you could improve. This not only provides valuable insights but also shows the customer that you value their opinion.

Follow up proactively: If you know there's been an issue (like a delayed delivery or a packaging problem), reach out to affected customers before they complain. This proactive approach can prevent many complaints and show customers that you're on top of potential problems.

CHAPTER 9
SCALING YOUR BUSINESS

Growth Strategies

As your meal prep business gains traction, the next exciting challenge is to scale and expand your operations. Growth is not just about increasing sales; it's about strategically expanding your reach, diversifying your offerings, and strengthening your market position.

Expanding Your Menu

Seasonal offerings

As your meal prep business grows, expanding your menu becomes a crucial strategy for attracting new customers and keeping existing ones engaged. One effective way to do this involves introducing seasonal offerings. These limited-time meals can create excitement and give customers a reason to keep coming back to see what's new.

Seasonal offerings take advantage of ingredients that are at their peak during specific times of the year. For example, in the summer, you might feature dishes with fresh berries, tomatoes, and zucchini. In the fall, pumpkin, squash, and apple-based meals could take center stage. Winter might bring hearty stews and roasted root vegetables, while spring could showcase asparagus, peas, and light, refreshing salads.

By aligning your menu with the seasons, you can offer several benefits to your customers:

Freshness: Seasonal ingredients are often at their peak flavor and nutritional value. This can result in tastier, more nutritious meals that your customers will love.

Variety: Changing your menu with the seasons prevents menu fatigue. Customers who might get bored with the same options all year round will have new dishes to look forward to each season.

Cost-effectiveness: Seasonal produce is often more abundant and therefore less expensive. This can help you maintain your profit margins while offering high-quality meals.

Sustainability: Using seasonal, locally-sourced ingredients can reduce the environmental impact of your business, which may appeal to eco-conscious customers.

To implement seasonal offerings effectively:

Plan ahead: Start developing your seasonal menus well in advance. This gives you time to perfect recipes, source ingredients, and market your new offerings.

Be flexible: Weather patterns can affect crop availability. Have backup plans in case certain ingredients aren't available when you expect them to be.

Educate your customers: Use your marketing channels to explain the benefits of seasonal eating. Share information about the ingredients you're using and why they're special.

Create anticipation: Tease upcoming seasonal menus to get customers excited. You could even run polls on social media to let customers vote on which seasonal dishes they'd like to see.

Consider themed menus: Align your seasonal offerings with holidays or local events. For example, you could offer special meals for Valentine's Day in February or create dishes inspired by a local food festival.

Test and refine: Use customer feedback to improve your seasonal offerings each year. The dishes that perform well can become annual traditions that customers look forward to.

New dietary options

In addition to seasonal offerings, expanding your menu to include new dietary options can help you reach a wider audience and cater to evolving customer needs. As awareness of various dietary requirements and preferences grows, offering a diverse range of options can set your meal prep business apart.

Consider adding or expanding these dietary options:

Vegetarian and Vegan: Plant-based diets are becoming increasingly popular. Offer creative, protein-rich meals that appeal not just to vegetarians and vegans, but also to flexitarians who are trying to reduce their meat consumption.

Gluten-free: Many people avoid gluten due to celiac disease, gluten sensitivity, or personal preference. Ensure you have a selection of tasty gluten-free options.

Keto and Low-carb: These diets remain popular for weight loss and health reasons. Develop meals that are high in healthy fats and proteins while low in carbohydrates.

Paleo: This diet focuses on foods that our ancestors might have eaten, such as meats, fish, fruits, and vegetables, while avoiding processed foods, grains, and dairy.

Mediterranean: Known for its health benefits, this diet emphasizes fruits, vegetables, whole grains, lean proteins, and healthy fats like olive oil.

Allergen-free: Create meals free from common allergens like nuts, dairy, or soy. Clearly label these meals to make it easy for customers with allergies to find safe options.

When expanding into new dietary options:

Educate yourself: Thoroughly research each diet to understand its principles and restrictions. This knowledge will help you create authentic, satisfying meals for each dietary category.

Train your staff: Ensure your kitchen staff understands the requirements of each diet and the importance of avoiding cross-contamination.

Label clearly: Make it easy for customers to identify which meals fit their dietary needs. Use clear, consistent labeling on your menu and packaging.

Seek certification: For options like gluten-free, consider getting certified. This can increase customer trust in your offerings.

Gather feedback: Ask customers following these diets for their input. They can provide valuable insights on what they're looking for in prepared meals.

Balance your menu: While offering diverse options, make sure your menu remains manageable for your kitchen to produce efficiently.

By expanding your menu with both seasonal offerings and new dietary options, you can keep your meal prep business fresh and appealing to a wide range of customers. This approach not only attracts new customers but also encourages existing ones to order more frequently, trying new options as you introduce them.

Geographic Expansion

New delivery areas

As your meal prep business grows and establishes a solid customer base, expanding into new delivery areas can be a natural next step. This expansion allows you to reach more potential customers and increase your revenue. However, it requires careful planning and execution to ensure success.

Before expanding your delivery area, conduct thorough market research. Identify areas with demographics similar to your current successful locations. Look for neighborhoods with a high concentration of your target customer profile - perhaps young professionals, health-conscious families, or fitness enthusiasts.

Consider the logistical challenges of expanding your delivery area. As you cover a larger geographic region, you'll need to ensure that you can maintain the quality and temperature of your meals during longer delivery times. This might involve investing in better insulation for your delivery containers or partnering with a refrigerated delivery service.

Evaluate your current kitchen capacity. Can it handle the increased volume of orders that will come with a larger delivery area? If not, you might need to expand your kitchen facilities or consider renting additional kitchen space closer to your new delivery areas.

Adjust your delivery pricing structure as needed. Longer delivery distances may increase your costs, which you'll need to factor into your pricing. Consider implementing a tiered delivery fee structure based on distance or setting a minimum order amount for free delivery to more distant areas.

As you expand, you'll likely need to hire additional delivery drivers. Ensure they are well-trained not just in efficient route planning, but also in customer service, as they'll be the face of your company for many customers.

Update your website and marketing materials to reflect your expanded service area. Make it easy for potential customers to check if you deliver to their location. You might consider creating a zip code checker on your website for this purpose.

Launch your expansion with a marketing campaign targeted at your new delivery areas. This could include social media ads geo-targeted to the new neighborhoods, direct mail campaigns, or partnerships with local businesses or community organizations.

Monitor the performance of your new delivery areas closely. Track metrics like order volume, customer acquisition cost, and customer retention rates. Be prepared to adjust your strategy if certain areas aren't performing as well as expected.

Consider phasing your expansion, starting with areas closest to your current delivery zone and gradually moving outward. This allows you to test and refine your expanded delivery processes before taking on the challenges of serving more distant areas.

Opening additional locations

While expanding your delivery area can help you reach more customers, opening additional physical locations can take your meal prep business to the next level. This strategy can help you serve a much larger geographic area and potentially enter new markets entirely.

The first step in opening a new location is choosing the right area. Look for locations that have a high concentration of your target demographic but are far enough from your existing location to avoid cannibalizing your current business. Consider factors like local competition, accessibility, and the availability of suitable commercial kitchen spaces.

Conduct a thorough financial analysis before committing to a new location. Consider all the costs involved, including rent, equipment, staffing, and marketing. Create detailed financial projections to ensure the new location will be profitable within a reasonable timeframe.

Securing funding for your expansion might be necessary. This could involve taking out a business loan, seeking investors, or reinvesting profits from your existing location. Make sure you have a solid business plan to present to potential lenders or investors.

When setting up your new location, strive for consistency with your existing operation. This includes the layout of your kitchen, your food preparation processes, and your quality control measures. However, be open to making adjustments based on lessons learned from your first location.

Staffing your new location is crucial. You might consider transferring some experienced staff from your original location to help train new employees and ensure consistency in your operations. Develop a comprehensive training program to bring new staff up to speed quickly.

Update your business processes to accommodate multiple locations. This might involve implementing new inventory management systems, centralizing certain administrative functions, or adopting new communication tools to keep all locations coordinated.

Consider how you'll manage your brand across multiple locations. Will each location have its own social media accounts, or will you manage everything centrally? How will you ensure consistent messaging and customer experience across all locations?

Launch your new location with fanfare. Host a grand opening event, offer special promotions, and leverage local media to generate buzz. Encourage customers from your original location to try out the new one if it's convenient for them.

As your new location gets up and running, closely monitor its performance. Compare key metrics like sales, customer satisfaction, and operational efficiency with your original location. Be prepared to make adjustments as needed to ensure the success of your new venture.

Opening additional locations can be a significant undertaking, but it also offers the potential for substantial growth. With careful planning and execution, you can successfully expand your meal prep business to serve a much larger customer base.

Partnerships and Collaborations

Corporate partnerships

Forming partnerships with corporations can provide a significant boost to your meal prep business. These collaborations can open up new revenue streams, increase your customer base, and enhance your brand's visibility. Corporate partnerships can take various forms, each offering unique benefits.

One common type of corporate partnership involves providing meal prep services to employees as a company benefit. Many businesses are increasingly focused on employee wellness, and offering healthy, convenient meal options can be an attractive perk. You could propose a program where the company subsidizes meal prep orders for their employees, or offer exclusive discounts to employees of partner companies.

To pursue this type of partnership:

Identify potential corporate partners: Look for companies in your area that align with your brand values and have a workforce that matches your target demographic.

Develop a compelling pitch: Highlight the benefits of your meal prep service for both the company and its employees. Emphasize how your service can contribute to employee wellness, productivity, and satisfaction.

Create customized offerings: Consider developing special meal plans or options tailored to the needs of each corporate partner. This could include meals designed for late-night shifts, options that cater to specific dietary requirements common in the company, or branded packaging for corporate events.

Offer flexible payment options: Some companies might prefer to fully subsidize meals for their employees, while others might want to offer a partial subsidy or simply provide your service as a discounted option. Be prepared to accommodate different arrangements.

Provide excellent customer service: Assign a dedicated account manager to each corporate client to ensure smooth communication and quick resolution of any issues.

Another form of corporate partnership could involve collaborating with local gyms, fitness studios, or wellness centers. These businesses often have clientele who are health-conscious and might be interested in convenient, nutritious meal options. You could offer exclusive discounts to members of these facilities, or even set up a pickup point at the location for added convenience.

For gym partnerships:

Align your meals with fitness goals: Develop meal plans that complement different workout regimens or fitness objectives.

Educate gym members: Offer to conduct workshops or seminars at the gym about the importance of nutrition in fitness, showcasing how your meals can support their goals.

Cross-promote: Feature the gym in your marketing materials and vice versa. This can help both businesses reach new potential customers.

Corporate catering is another avenue to explore. While this might require some adjustments to your usual meal prep model, it can be a lucrative addition to your business. You could offer healthy catering options for corporate meetings, events, or conferences.

For corporate catering:

Develop a separate menu: Create options suitable for group settings, such as platters or buffet-style meals.

Invest in catering equipment: You may need to purchase items like chafing dishes or large-scale transport containers.

Train staff: Catering often requires different skills than individual meal prep. Ensure your team is prepared to handle larger-scale food preparation and service.

Influencer collaborations

In today's digital age, influencer collaborations can be a powerful way to expand your meal prep business's reach and credibility. Influencers, particularly those focused on health, fitness, or lifestyle content, can introduce your brand to their engaged followers and provide social proof for your products.

When considering influencer collaborations:

Choose the right influencers: Look for influencers whose audience aligns with your target market. They should have a genuine interest in health and nutrition, and their content style should match your brand's tone.

Start local: Begin by partnering with influencers in your local area. They can provide authentic reviews of your service, including the delivery experience.

Consider micro-influencers: While they have smaller followings, micro-influencers often have highly engaged audiences and can be more cost-effective than larger influencers.

Develop a clear agreement: Outline expectations, deliverables, and compensation clearly. This might include the number of posts, specific messaging points, or exclusivity clauses.

Provide a great experience: Send influencers a variety of your best meals. Consider creating a special "influencer package" that showcases the range of your offerings.

Encourage authentic content: While you can provide guidelines, allow influencers some creative freedom. Authentic, personal content often resonates more with audiences than overly scripted promotions.

Track results: Use unique discount codes or landing pages for each influencer to track the effectiveness of these collaborations.

Consider long-term partnerships: Building ongoing relationships with a few key influencers can be more effective than one-off collaborations with many.

Some ideas for influencer collaborations include:

Meal plan challenge: Partner with an influencer to promote a week-long or month-long challenge using your meal prep service.

Recipe collaboration: Work with a food-focused influencer to create a special menu item, then feature it as a limited-time offering.

Day-in-the-life content: Have an influencer document how your meal prep service fits into and improves their daily routine.

Live unboxing or tasting: Engage audiences with real-time content as an influencer tries your meals for the first time.

Behind-the-scenes tour: Invite an influencer to your kitchen to see how meals are prepared, emphasizing your commitment to quality and food safety.

By leveraging both corporate partnerships and influencer collaborations, you can significantly expand the reach and appeal of your meal prep business. These strategies not only help you acquire new customers but also build credibility and trust in your brand, setting the stage for long-term growth and success.

CHAPTER 10
FINANCIAL MANAGEMENT

Budgeting and Forecasting

Mastering the financial aspects of your meal prep business is crucial for long-term success and sustainable growth. Effective budgeting and forecasting allow you to make informed decisions, allocate resources wisely, and navigate the financial landscape with confidence.

Creating a Budget

Fixed and variable costs

A well-structured budget serves as the backbone of a thriving meal prep business. Grasping the nuances between fixed and variable costs empowers entrepreneurs to craft precise financial plans and make data-driven decisions that propel their venture forward.

Fixed costs maintain consistency regardless of production volume. In the context of a meal prep business, these expenses typically encompass rent for kitchen facilities, equipment leases, insurance coverage, and base salaries for full-time personnel. Let's dissect some common fixed costs in greater detail:

Rent for commercial kitchen space: $2,000 per month

This cost covers a 1,000 square foot commercial kitchen in a mid-tier urban area. The space includes basic amenities such as water, gas, and electricity connections.

Equipment lease: $500 per month

This encompasses leasing arrangements for essential equipment like industrial ovens, refrigerators, and food processors. Leasing often proves more cost-effective for startups compared to outright purchases.

Insurance: $300 per month

This amount covers general liability insurance, property insurance, and workers' compensation. Adequate coverage protects the business from potential lawsuits and unforeseen incidents.

Base salaries: $5,000 per month

This accounts for the wages of two full-time employees: a head chef ($3,500) and a kitchen assistant ($1,500). These salaries remain constant regardless of production levels.

Total fixed costs: $7,800 per month

Variable costs fluctuate in direct proportion to production levels. These expenses include ingredients, packaging materials, utilities, and part-time labor. As meal production increases, so do variable costs. Here's a detailed breakdown of variable costs per meal:

Ingredients: $3.50

This covers the cost of high-quality, fresh ingredients for a balanced meal, including proteins, vegetables, grains, and seasonings.

Packaging: $0.75

This includes eco-friendly containers, labels, and any additional packaging materials required for safe food transport.

Labor (per meal): $1.25

This accounts for part-time staff hired during peak production periods, calculated based on the average time taken to prepare each meal.

Utilities (per meal): $0.50

This covers the additional electricity, gas, and water usage directly attributed to meal production.

Total variable cost per meal: $6.00

To calculate the total variable cost for a month, multiply the per-meal cost by the number of meals produced. For example, if the business produces 1,000 meals in a month:

Total variable cost = $6.00 x 1,000 = $6,000

By combining fixed and variable costs, we gain a comprehensive view of monthly expenses:

Total monthly costs = Fixed costs + Variable costs

Total monthly costs = $7,800 + $6,000 = $13,800

A thorough understanding of these costs aids in setting appropriate prices and determining the break-even point. The break-even point represents the number of meals that must be sold to cover all costs. Calculate it using this formula:

Break-even point = Fixed costs / (Price per meal - Variable cost per meal)

Assuming a selling price of $12 per meal:

Break-even point = $7,800 / ($12 - $6) = 1,300 meals

This calculation reveals that the business needs to sell 1,300 meals per month to cover all costs. Any sales beyond this point contribute directly to profit.

Cash flow management

Effective cash flow management ensures a meal prep business maintains sufficient liquidity to cover expenses and invest in growth opportunities. Several strategies can optimize cash flow:

Accounts receivable management: Implement clear, concise payment terms for customers. Offer incentives for early payment and establish penalties for late payments. For example, a 2% discount for payments made within 10 days can encourage prompt settlements. This approach might look like:

Invoice total: $1,000

2% discount if paid within 10 days: $20

Discounted total if paid early: $980

By offering this incentive, the business may receive payment faster, improving cash flow even with a slight reduction in revenue.

Accounts payable optimization: Negotiate favorable payment terms with suppliers. Aim for 30-day payment terms when possible, allowing the business to retain cash longer. However, balance this with maintaining good supplier relationships. For instance:

Invoice from supplier: $5,000

Negotiated terms: Net 30 (payment due in 30 days)

This arrangement allows the business to hold onto $5,000 for an additional 30 days, potentially earning interest or using the funds for short-term needs.

Inventory control: Implement a just-in-time inventory system to minimize tied-up cash. Use the Economic Order Quantity (EOQ) formula to determine optimal order sizes:

$$EOQ = \sqrt{[(2 \times \text{Annual demand} \times \text{Ordering cost}) / (\text{Annual holding cost per unit})]}$$

For example, if annual demand for a particular ingredient 10,000 units, ordering cost $50, and annual holding cost per unit $2:

$$EOQ = \sqrt{[(2 \times 10{,}000 \times \$50) / \$2]} = 707 \text{ units}$$

This calculation suggests ordering 707 units at a time minimizes total inventory costs, balancing ordering costs with storage expenses.

Cash flow forecasting: Develop a rolling 13-week cash flow forecast. Update it weekly to maintain accuracy. Here's a more detailed example:

Week 1:

Starting balance: $10,000

Cash inflows:

- Sales revenue: $7,500

- Account receivables collected: $500

Total inflows: $8,000

Cash outflows:

- Ingredient purchases: $3,000

- Rent: $2,000

- Salaries: $2,500

Total outflows: $7,500

Ending balance: $10,500

Week 2:

Starting balance: $10,500

Cash inflows:

- Sales revenue: $8,000

- Account receivables collected: $500

Total inflows: $8,500

Cash outflows:

- Ingredient purchases: $3,200
- Equipment lease payment: $500
- Utilities: $300
- Salaries: $4,000

Total outflows: $8,000

Ending balance: $11,000

Continue this process for all 13 weeks, adjusting projections based on actual results and new information. This detailed forecast helps anticipate cash shortages or surpluses, allowing for proactive financial management.

Working capital management: Maintain a healthy working capital ratio (current assets / current liabilities) between 1.2 and 2.0. For example:

Current assets:

- Cash: $20,000
- Accounts receivable: $15,000
- Inventory: $15,000

Total current assets: $50,000

Current liabilities:

- Accounts payable: $20,000
- Short-term debt: $10,000

Total current liabilities: $30,000

Working capital ratio = $50,000 / $30,000 = 1.67

This ratio indicates a strong short-term financial position, suggesting the business can comfortably meet its short-term obligations.

Emergency fund: Set aside 3-6 months of operating expenses in a separate account. For instance, if monthly expenses average $13,800, aim for an emergency fund of $41,400 to $82,800. This fund acts as a financial buffer against unexpected challenges or economic downturns.

By meticulously implementing these strategies and regularly reviewing financial performance, a meal prep business can maintain robust cash flow, navigate unexpected challenges, and capitalize on growth opportunities. Consistent monitoring and adjustment of budget and cash flow management practices contribute significantly to long-term success and sustainability in the competitive food service industry.

Financial Reporting

Profit and loss statements

Profit and loss statements, also known as income statements, serve as a financial report card for your meal prep business. They show how much money your business has made or lost over a specific period, typically a month, quarter, or year. By understanding these statements, you can make informed decisions about your business's future.

Let's break down a profit and loss statement for a meal prep business:

Revenue: This represents the total amount of money earned from selling meals. For example, if you sold 2,000 meals at $12 each in a month, your revenue would be:

Revenue = Number of meals sold × Price per meal

Revenue = 2,000 × $12 = $24,000

Cost of Goods Sold (COGS): These are the direct costs associated with producing your meals. They include ingredients, packaging, and direct labor. Using our previous example of $6 variable cost per meal:

COGS = Number of meals sold × Variable cost per meal

COGS = 2,000 × $6 = $12,000

Gross Profit: This shows how much money you've made after subtracting the cost of producing your meals from your revenue.

Gross Profit = Revenue - COGS

Gross Profit = $24,000 - $12,000 = $12,000

Operating Expenses: These are the costs of running your business that aren't directly tied to meal production. They include rent, utilities, marketing, and administrative salaries. Let's say these total $8,000 for the month.

Net Profit: This is the bottom line - how much money your business has made after all expenses have been paid.

Net Profit = Gross Profit - Operating Expenses

Net Profit = $12,000 - $8,000 = $4,000

Your profit and loss statement would look like this:

Revenue: $24,000

Cost of Goods Sold: $12,000

Gross Profit: $12,000

Operating Expenses: $8,000

Net Profit: $4,000

This statement tells you that your business made $4,000 in profit for the month. You can use this information to track your business's performance over time and make decisions about pricing, expenses, and growth strategies.

To analyze your profit and loss statement further, you can calculate some useful ratios:

Gross Profit Margin: This shows what percentage of your revenue remains after paying for the direct costs of producing your meals.

Gross Profit Margin = (Gross Profit ÷ Revenue) × 100

Gross Profit Margin = ($12,000 ÷ $24,000) × 100 = 50%

This means that for every dollar of sales, you keep 50 cents after paying for the direct costs of producing the meals.

Net Profit Margin: This shows what percentage of your revenue remains as profit after all expenses have been paid.

Net Profit Margin = (Net Profit ÷ Revenue) × 100

Net Profit Margin = ($4,000 ÷ $24,000) × 100 = 16.67%

This means that for every dollar of sales, about 17 cents remains as profit after all expenses have been paid.

By tracking these figures and ratios over time, you can spot trends in your business's performance and make informed decisions about how to improve profitability.

Balance sheets

A balance sheet provides a snapshot of your meal prep business's financial position at a specific point in time. It shows what your business owns (assets), what it owes (liabilities), and the owner's equity. Understanding your balance sheet helps you assess your business's financial health and make smart decisions about investments and financing.

Let's create a sample balance sheet for your meal prep business:

Assets: These are things your business owns that have value. They're typically divided into current assets (which can be converted to cash within a year) and non-current assets (which are long-term investments).

Current Assets:

Cash: $15,000

Accounts Receivable: $5,000 (money owed to you by customers)

Inventory: $3,000 (value of ingredients and packaging on hand)

Non-Current Assets:

Equipment: $20,000 (value of kitchen equipment)

Vehicle: $15,000 (for meal deliveries)

Total Assets: $58,000

Liabilities: These are amounts your business owes to others. They're also divided into current liabilities (due within a year) and non-current liabilities (long-term debts).

Current Liabilities:

Accounts Payable: $4,000 (money you owe suppliers)

Short-term Loan: $5,000

Non-Current Liabilities:

Long-term Loan: $20,000 (for equipment purchase)

Total Liabilities: $29,000

Owner's Equity: This represents the owner's investment in the business plus retained earnings (profits that have been reinvested in the business).

Owner's Investment: $25,000

Retained Earnings: $4,000

Total Owner's Equity: $29,000

Your balance sheet would look like this:

Assets:

Current Assets:

Cash: $15,000

Accounts Receivable: $5,000

Inventory: $3,000

Non-Current Assets:

Equipment: $20,000

Vehicle: $15,000

Total Assets: $58,000

Liabilities:

Current Liabilities:

Accounts Payable: $4,000

Short-term Loan: $5,000

Non-Current Liabilities:

Long-term Loan: $20,000

Total Liabilities: $29,000

Owner's Equity:

Owner's Investment: $25,000

Retained Earnings: $4,000

Total Owner's Equity: $29,000

Total Liabilities and Owner's Equity: $58,000

The balance sheet should always balance, meaning that Total Assets should equal Total Liabilities plus Owner's Equity. This is known as the accounting equation:

Assets = Liabilities + Owner's Equity

$58,000 = $29,000 + $29,000

To analyze your balance sheet, you can calculate some useful ratios:

Current Ratio: This measures your ability to pay short-term obligations.

Current Ratio = Current Assets ÷ Current Liabilities

Current Ratio = $23,000 ÷ $9,000 = 2.56

A current ratio above 1 indicates that you have enough current assets to cover your current liabilities. In this case, you have $2.56 in current assets for every $1 of current liabilities, which is a healthy position.

Debt-to-Equity Ratio: This shows how much of your business is financed through debt versus owner's equity.

Debt-to-Equity Ratio = Total Liabilities ÷ Owner's Equity

Debt-to-Equity Ratio = $29,000 ÷ $29,000 = 1

A ratio of 1 means that your business has an equal amount of debt and equity financing. Generally, a lower ratio is considered less risky, but the ideal ratio can vary by industry.

These reports help you track your progress, identify areas for improvement, and make informed decisions about the future of your business. Remember to update these reports regularly and seek professional advice if you're unsure about any aspects of your financial reporting.

Funding and Investment

Bootstrapping

Bootstrapping your meal prep business means starting and growing it using your own resources, without relying on external funding. This approach gives you complete control over your business and allows you to build it at your own pace. However, it also means you'll need to be creative and resourceful with your limited funds.

To bootstrap effectively, start small and focus on minimizing costs while maximizing revenue. Begin by operating from your home kitchen if local regulations allow. This eliminates the need for costly commercial kitchen rent. As you grow, you can reinvest your profits into the business to expand.

Let's look at a practical example of bootstrapping a meal prep business:

Initial investment (from personal savings): $5,000

Expenses:

Kitchen equipment: $2,000

Initial ingredients and packaging: $1,500

Marketing (website and social media): $500

Licenses and permits: $500

Reserve for unexpected costs: $500

Total initial expenses: $5,000

In this scenario, you've used your entire initial investment to set up the business. Now, you need to generate enough revenue to cover ongoing expenses and eventually turn a profit.

Assume you can produce and sell 50 meals per week at $10 each:

Weekly revenue: 50 meals × $10 = $500

Monthly revenue: $500 × 4 weeks = $2,000

Your monthly expenses might look like this:

Ingredients and packaging: $800

Utilities: $100

Marketing: $100

Total monthly expenses: $1,000

Monthly profit: $2,000 - $1,000 = $1,000

By reinvesting this $1,000 monthly profit back into the business, you can gradually expand your operations. For example, after three months, you'd have $3,000 to invest in better equipment or to rent a small commercial kitchen space.

Bootstrapping requires patience and careful financial management. Track every dollar spent and earned. Use this formula to calculate your runway - how long your current funds will last:

Runway = Available funds ÷ Monthly burn rate

For example, if you have $5,000 in the bank and your monthly expenses (burn rate) are $1,000:

Runway = $5,000 ÷ $1,000 = 5 months

This means you have 5 months to become profitable before running out of money. By keeping a close eye on this metric, you can make informed decisions about when to expand or when to cut costs.

Seeking investors or loans

While bootstrapping offers control and independence, it can limit your growth potential. Seeking external funding through investors or loans can provide the capital needed to scale your meal prep business more quickly.

Investors: Angel investors or venture capitalists can provide significant funding in exchange for equity in your business. To attract investors, you'll need a solid business plan and financial projections.

Let's say you're seeking $100,000 in exchange for 20% equity in your business. You'd need to convince investors that your business will be worth at least $500,000 in the near future. Here's how you might project this growth:

Current annual revenue: $24,000 (from our bootstrapping example)

Projected annual revenue after investment: $240,000 (10x growth)

Projected net profit margin: 15%

Projected annual profit: $240,000 × 15% = $36,000

If investors expect a 10x return on their investment within 5 years, you'd need to show how your business could be valued at $1,000,000 or more. One common valuation method is the multiple of earnings approach:

Business valuation = Annual profit × Earnings multiple

Assuming an earnings multiple of 30 (common for high-growth businesses):

Business valuation = $36,000 × 30 = $1,080,000

This valuation would provide the 10x return investors are looking for on their $100,000 investment.

Loans: Business loans from banks or alternative lenders can provide capital without giving up equity. However, you'll need to repay the loan with interest.

For example, let's say you secure a $50,000 loan at 10% annual interest, to be repaid over 5 years. Your monthly payment would be approximately $1,062. This means over the course of 5 years, you'd pay a total of about $63,720, with $13,720 going towards interest.

To justify this loan, your business plan should show how this $50,000 investment will generate more than $13,720 in additional profits over 5 years. This could come from increased production capacity, better equipment, or expanded marketing efforts.

When deciding between bootstrapping and seeking external funding, consider these factors:

Growth rate: How quickly do you want to expand?

Control: Are you willing to give up some control to investors?

Risk tolerance: Can you take on debt, or do you prefer the lower risk of bootstrapping?

Market opportunity: Is there a time-sensitive opportunity that requires rapid scaling?

By carefully weighing these factors and running the numbers, you can make an informed decision about the best funding strategy for your meal prep business. Remember, many successful businesses use a combination of bootstrapping and external funding as they grow, adapting their approach to meet changing needs and opportunities.

For example, you might start by bootstrapping for the first year, reinvesting all profits to prove your business model. Once you have a track record of success, you could then approach investors or lenders with a stronger case for funding, potentially securing better terms or larger amounts of capital.

Whichever path you choose, always keep a close eye on your finances. Regularly update your financial projections and be prepared to adjust your strategy as your business grows and evolves.

www.ingramcontent.com/pod-product-compliance
Lightning Source LLC
Chambersburg PA
CBHW072051230526
45479CB00010B/668